Love's Cure
by Francis Beaumont, John Fletcher & Philip Massinger

or, The Martial Maid

A COMEDY

The English dramatists Francis Beaumont and John Fletcher, collaborated in their writing during the reign of James I of England (James VI of Scotland, 1567–1625; in England he reigned from 1603).

Beaumont & Fletcher began to collaborate as writers soon after they met. After notable failures of their solo works their first joint effort, Philaster, was a success and tragicomedy was the genre they explored and built upon. There would be many further successes to follow.

There is an account that at the time the two men shared everything. They lived together in a house on the Bankside in Southwark, "they also lived together in Bankside, sharing clothes and having one wench in the house between them." Or as another account puts it "sharing everything in the closest intimacy."

Whatever the truth of this they were now recognised as perhaps the best writing team of their generation, so much so, that their joint names was applied to all the works in which either, or both, had a pen including those with Philip Massinger, James Shirley and Nathan Field.

The first Beaumont and Fletcher folio of 1647 contained 35 plays; 53 plays were included in the second folio in 1679. Other works bring the total plays in the canon to about 55. However there appears here to have been some duplicity on the account of the publishers who seemed to attribute so many to the team. It is now thought that the work between solely by Beaumont and Fletcher amounts to approximately 15 plays, though of course further works by them were re-worked by others and the originals lost.

After Beaumont's early death in 1616 Fletcher continued to write and, at his height was, by many standards, the equal of Shakespeare in popularity until his own death in 1625.

Philip Massinger worked several times with Beaumont & Fletcher and many times with Fletcher after Beaumont's death. Whilst he too collaborated with various other playwrights he also has approximately 16 plays to his solo credit though most of these were lost when used by a kitchen cook to start a fire.

Index of Contents

DRAMATIS PERSONAE
MEN
Assistant, or Governor.
Vitelli, a young Gentleman, enemy to Alvarez.
Lamoral, a fighting Gallant, friend to Vitelli.
Anastro, an honest Gentleman, friend to Vitelli.
Don Alvarez, a noble Gent. Father to Lucio, and Clara.
Syavedra, a friend to Alvarez.
Lucio, Son to Alvarez, a brave young Gent, in womans habit.
Alguazeir, a sharking panderly Constable.
Pachieco, a Cobler   }
Mendoza, a Botcher   } of worship.
Metaldie, a Smith   }
Lazarillo, Pachieco his hungry servant.
Bobbadilla, a witty knave, servant to Eugenia, and Steward
Servant to Alvarez.
Herald.
Officer.
WOMEN
Eugenia, a virtuous Lady, wife to Don Alvarez.
Clara, Daughter to Eugenia, a martial Maid, valiant and chaste, enamoured of Vitelli.

Genevora, Sister to Vitelli, in love with Lucio.
Malroda, a wanton Mistriss of Vitelli.

LOVE'S CURE

A PROLOGUE (At the reviving of this Play)

Statues and Pictures challenge price and fame;
If they can justly boast, and prove they came
From Phidias or Apelles. None denie,
Poets and Painters hold a sympathy;
Yet their works may decay, and lose their grace,
Receiving blemish in their Limbs or Face.
When the Minds Art has this preheminence,
She still retaineth her first excellence.
Then why should not this dear Piece be esteem'd
Child to the richest fancies that e'r teem'd?
When not their meanest off-spring, that came forth,
But bore the image of their Fathers worth.
Beaumonts, and Fletchers, whose desert out-wayes
The best applause, and their least sprig of Bayes
Is worthy Phæbus; and who comes to gather
Their fruits of wit, he shall not rob the treasure.
Nor can you ever surfeit of the plenty,
Nor can you call them rare, though they be dainty.
The more you take, the more you do them right,
And we will thank you for your own delight.

ACTUS PRIMUS

SCÆNA PRIMA

Enter **VITELLI, LAMORAL, ANASTRO**.

VITELLI
Alvarez pardon'd?

ANASTRO
And return'd

LAMORAL
I saw him land

At St. Lucars, and such a general welcome,
Fame as harbinger to his brave actions,
Had with the easie people, prepar'd for him,
As if by his command alone, and fortune
Holland, with those low Provinces, that hold out
Against the Arch-Duke, were again compell'd
With their obedience to give up their lives
To be at his Devotion.

VITELLI
You amaze me,
For though I have heard, that when he fled from Sevil
To save his life (then forfeited to Law
For murth'ring Don Pedro my dear Uncle)
His extream wants enforc'd him to take pay
I'th' Army, sate down then before Ostend,
'Twas never yet reported, by whose favour
He durst presume to entertain a thought
Of coming home with pardon.

ANASTRO
'Tis our nature
Or not to hear, or not to give belief
To what we wish far from our enemies.

LAMORAL
Sir, 'tis most certain, the Infanta's Letters
Assisted by the Arch-Dukes, to King Philip,
Have not alone secur'd him from the rigor
Of our Castilian Justice, but return'd him
A free man and in grace.

VITELLI
By what curs'd means
Could such a fugitive arise unto
The knowledge of their Highnesses? much more
(Though known) to stand but in the least degree
Of favour with them?

LAMORAL
To give satisfaction
To your demand, though to praise him I hate,
Can yield me small contentment, I will tell you,
And truly, since should I detract his worth,
'Twould argue want of merit in my self.
Briefly to pass his tedious pilgrimage
For sixteen years, a banish'd guilty man,
And to forget the storms, th' affrights, the horrors

His constancy, not fortune, overcame,
I bring him, with his little son, grown man
(Though 'twas said here, he took a Daughter with him)
To Ostend's bloody siege that stage of war,
Wherein the flower of many Nations acted,
And the whole Christian world spectators were;
There by his Son, or were he by adoption,
Or nature his, a brave Scene was presented,
Which I make choice to speak of, since from that
The good success of Alvarez, had beginning.

VITELLI
So I love virtue in an enemy
That I desire in the relation of
This young mans glorious deed, you'ld keep your self
A friend to truth, and it.

LAMORAL
Such was my purpose;
The Town being oft assaulted, but in vain,
To dare the proud defendents to a sally,
Weary of ease, Don Inigo Peralta,
Son to the General of our Castile forces,
All arm'd, advanc'd within shot of their Walls,
From whence the Musquetiers plaid thick upon him,
Yet he (brave youth) as careless of the danger,
As careful of his honor, drew his sword,
And waving it about his head, as if
He dar'd one spirited like himself, to trial
Of single valor, he made his retreat
With such a slow, and yet majestique pace,
As if he still call'd loud, dare none come on?
When sodainly, from a postern of the Town
Two gallant horsemen issued, and o'ertook him,
The Army looking on, yet not a man
That durst relieve the rash adventurer,
Which Lucio, son to Alvarez then seeing,
As in the Vant-guard he sate bravely mounted,
Or were it pity of the youths misfortune,
Care to preserve the honor of his Countrey,
Or bold desire to get himself a name,
He made his brave Horse like a whirlwind bear him,
Among the Combatants: and in a moment
Discharg'd his Petronel, with such sure aim
That of the adverse party from his horse,
One tumbled dead, then wheeling round, and drawing
A Faulcion, swift as lightning he came on
Upon the other, and with one strong blow,

In view of the amazed Town, and Camp,
He struck him dead, and brought Peralta off
With double honor to himself.

VITELLI
'Twas brave:
But the success of this?

LAMORAL
The Camp receiv'd him
With acclamations of joy and welcome,
And for addition to the fair reward
Being a massy chain of Gold given to him
By young Peralta's Father, he was brought
To the Infanta's presence, kiss'd her hand,
And from that Lady, (greater in her goodness
Than her high birth) had this encouragement:
Go on young man; yet not to feed thy valour
With hope of recompence to come, from me,
For present satisfaction of what's past,
Ask any thing that's fit for me to give,
And thee to take, and be assur'd of it.

ANASTRO
Excellent Princess.

VITELLI
And stil'd worthily
The heart-bloud, nay the Soul of Soldiers.
But what was his request?

LAMORAL
That the repeal
Of Alvarez makes plain: he humbly begg'd
His Fathers pardon, and so movingly
Told the sad story of your Uncles death
That the Infanta wept, and instantly
Granting his suit, working the Arch-Duke to it,
Their Letters were directed to the King,
With whom they so prevail'd, that Alvarez
Was freely pardon'd.

VITELLI
'Tis not in the King
To make that good.

ANASTRO
Not in the King? what subject

Dares contradict his power?

VITELLI
In this I dare,
And will: and not call his prerogative
In question, nor presume to limit it.
I know he is the Master of his Laws,
And may forgive the forfeits made to them,
But not the injury done to my honor;
And since (forgetting my brave Uncles merits
And many services, under Duke D' Alva)
He suffers him to fall, wresting from Justice
The powerful sword, that would revenge his death,
I'll fill with this Astrea's empty hand,
And in my just wreak, make this arm the Kings,
My deadly hate to Alvarez, and his house,
Which as I grew in years, hath still encreas'd,
As if it call'd on time to make me man,
Slept while it had no object for her fury
But a weak woman, and her talk'd of Daughter:
But now, since there are quarries, worth her sight
Both in the father, and his hopeful son,
I'll boldly cast her off, and gorge her full
With both their hearts: to further which, your friendship,
And oaths: will your assistance, let your deeds
Make answer to me: useless are all words
Till you have writ performance with your swords.

[Exeunt.

SCÆNA SECUNDA

Enter **BOBADILLA** and **LUCIO**.

LUCIO
Go fetch my work: this Ruffe was not well starch'd,
So tell the maid, 't has too much blew in it,
And look you that the Partridge and the Pullen
Have clean meat, and fresh water, or my Mother
Is like to hear on't.

BOBADILLA
Oh good St. Jaques help me: was there ever such an Hermaphrodite heard of? would any wench living, that should hear and see what I do, be wrought to believe, that the best of a man lies under this Petticoat, and that a Codpiece were far fitter here, than a Pinn'd Placket?

LUCIO
You had best talk filthily: do; I have a tongue
To tell my Mother, as well as ears to hear
Your ribaldry.

BOBADILLA
Nay you have ten womens tongues that way I am sure: why my young Master or Mistriss, Madam, Don, or what you will, what the devil have you to do with Pullen, or Partridge? or to sit pricking on a clout all day? you have a better needle, I know, and might make better work, if you had grace to use it.

LUCIO
Why, how dare you speak this before me, sirrah?

BOBADILLA
Nay rather, why dare not you do what I speak?—though my Lady your mother, for fear of Vitelli and his faction, hath brought you up like her Daughter, and has kept you these 20 years, which is ever since you were born, a close prisoner within doors, yet since you are a man, and are as well provided as other men are, methinks you should have the same motions of the flesh, as other Cavaliers of us are inclin'd unto.

LUCIO
Indeed you have cause to love those wanton motions,
They having hope you to an excellent whipping,
For doing something, I but put you in mind of it,
With the Indian Maid, the Governor sent my mother
From Mexico.

BOBADILLA
Why, I but taught her a Spanish trick in charity, and holpe the King to a subject that may live to take Grave Maurice prisoner, and that was more good to the State, than a thousand such as you are ever like to doe: and I will tell you, (in a fatherly care of the Infant I speak it) if he live (as bless the babe, in passion I remember him) to your years, shall he spend his time in pinning, painting, purling, and perfuming as you do? no, he shall to the wars, use his Spanish Pike, though with the danger of the lash, as his father has done, and when he is provoked, as I am now, draw his Toledo desperately, as—

LUCIO
You will not kill me? oh.

BOBADILLA
I knew this would silence him: how he hides his eies!
If he were a wench now, as he seems, what an advantage
Had I, drawing two Toledo's, when one can do this!
But oh me, my Lady: I must put up: young Master
I did but jest: Oh custom, what hast thou made of him?

[Enter **EUGENIA** and **SERVANTS**.

EUGENIA
For bringing this, be still my friend; no more

A servant to me.

BOBADILLA
What's the matter?

EUGENIA
Here,
Even here, where I am happy to receive
Assurance of my Alvarez return,
I will kneel down: and may those holy thoughts
That now possess me wholly, make this place
A Temple to me, where I may give thanks
For this unhop'd for blessing Heavens kind hand
Hath pour'd upon me.

LUCIO
Let my duty Madam
Presume, if you have cause of joy, to intreat
I may share in it.

BOBADILLA
'Tis well, he has forgot how I frighted him yet.

EUGENIA
Thou shalt: but first kneel with me Lucio,
No more Posthumia now, thou hast a Father,
A Father living to take off that name,
Which my too credulous fears, that he was dead,
Bestow'd upon thee: thou shalt see him Lucio
And make him young again, by seeing thee,
Who only hadst a being in my Womb
When he went from me, Lucio: Oh my joyes,
So far transport me, that I must forget
The ornaments of Matrons, modesty,
And grave behaviour; but let all forgive me
If in th' expression of my soul's best comfort
Though old, I do a while forget mine age
And play the wanton in the entertainment
Of those delights I have so long despair'd of.

LUCIO
Shall I then see my Father?

EUGENIA
This hour Lucio;
Which reckon the beginning of thy life
I mean that life, in which thou shalt appear
To be such as I brought thee forth, a man,

This womanish disguise, in which I have
So long conceal'd thee, thou shalt now cast off,
And change those qualities thou didst learn from me,
For masculine virtues, for which seek no tutor,
But let thy fathers actions be thy precepts;
And for thee Zancho, now expect reward
For thy true service.

BOBADILLA
Shall I? you hear fellow Stephano, learn to know
me more respectively; how dost thou think I shall become
the Stewards chair, ha? will not these slender hanches show
well with a chain, and a gold night-Cap after supper, when
I take the accompts?

EUGENIA
Haste, and take down those Blacks with which my chamber
Hath like the widow, her sad Mistriss mourn'd,
And hang up for it, the rich Persian Arras,
Us'd on my wedding night, for this to me
Shall be a second marriage: send for Musique,
And will the Cooks to use their best of cunning
To please the palat.

BOBADILLA
Will your Ladyship have a Potato-pie, 'tis a good
stirring dish for an old Lady, after a long Lent.

EUGENIA
Begone I say: why Sir, you can goe faster?

BOBADILLA
I could Madam: but I am now to practise the
Stewards pace, that's the reward I look for: every man must
fashion his gate, according to his calling: you fellow Stephano,
may walk faster, to overtake preferment: so, usher me.

LUCIO
Pray Madam, let the wastcoat I last wrought
Be made up for my Father: I will have
A Cap, and Boot-hose sutable to it.

EUGENIA
Of that
We'll think hereafter Lucio: our thoughts now
Must have no object but thy Fathers welcome,
To which thy help—

LUCIO
With humble gladness, Madam.

[Exeunt.

SCÆNA TERTIA

Enter **ALVAREZ**, **CLARA**.

ALVAREZ
Where lost we Syavedra?

CLARA
He was met
Ent'ring the City by some Gentlemen
Kinsmen, as he said of his own, with whom
For compliment sake (for so I think he term'd it)
He was compell'd to stay: though I much wonder
A man that knows to do, and has done well
In the head of his troop, when the bold foe charg'd home,
Can learn so sodainly to abuse his time
In apish entertainment: for my part
(By all the glorious rewards of war)
I had rather meet ten enemies in the field
All sworn to fetch my head, than be brought on
To change an hours discourse with one of these
Smooth City-fools, or Tissue-Cavaliers,
The only Gallants, as they wisely think,
To get a Jewel, or a wanton Kiss
From a Court-lip, though painted.

ALVAREZ
My Love Clara,
(For Lucio is a name thou must forget
With Lucio's bold behaviour) though thy breeding
I' th' Camp, may plead something in the excuse
Of thy rough manners, custom having chang'd,
Though not thy Sex, the softness of thy nature,
And fortune (then a cruel stepdame to thee)
Impos'd upon thy tender sweetness, burthens
Of hunger, cold, wounds, want, such as would crack
The sinews of a man, not born a Soldier:
Yet now she smiles, and like a natural mother
Looks gently on thee, Clara, entertain
Her proffer'd bounties with a willing bosom;
Thou shalt no more have need to use thy sword;

Thy beauty (which even Belgia hath not alter'd)
Shall be a stronger guard, to keep my Clara,
Than that has been, (though never us'd but nobly)
And know thus much.

CLARA
Sir, I know only that
It stands not with my duty to gain-say you,
In any thing: I must, and will put on
What fashion you think best: though I could wish
I were what I appear.

ALVAREZ
Endeavour rather

[Musick.

To be what you are, Clara, entring here,
As you were born, a woman.

[Enter **EUGENIA, LUCIO, SERVANTS**.

EUGENIA
Let choice Musick
In the best voice that e'er touch'd humane ear,
For joy hath ti'd my tongue up, speak your welcome.

ALVAREZ
My soul (for thou giv'st new life to my spirit)
Myriads of joyes, though short in number of
Thy virtues, fall on thee; Oh my Eugenia,
Th' assurance that I do embrace thee, makes
My twenty years of sorrow but a dream,
And by the Nectar, which I take from these,
I feel my age restor'd, and like old Æson
Grow young again.

EUGENIA
My Lord, long wish'd for welcome,
'Tis a sweet briefness, yet in that short word
All pleasures which I may call mine, begin,
And may they long increase, before they find
A second period: let mine eies now surfeit
On this so wish'd for object, and my lips
Yet modestly pay back the parting kiss
You trusted with them, when you fled from Sevil,
With little Clara my sweet daughter: lives she?
Yet I could chide my self, having you here

For being so covetous of all joyes at once,
T' enquire for her, you being alone, to me
My Clara, Lucio, my Lord, my self,
Nay more than all the world.

ALVAREZ
As you, to me are.

EUGENIA
Sit down, and let me feed upon the story
Of your past dangers, now you are here in safety
It will give rellish, and fresh appetite
To my delights, if such delights can cloy me.
Yet do not Alvarez, let me first yield you
Account of my life in your absence, and
Make you acquainted how I have preserv'd
The Jewel left lock'd up in my womb,
When you, in being forc'd to leave your Countrey,
Suffer'd a civil death.

[Within clashing swords.

ALVAREZ
Doe my Eugenia,
'Tis that I most desire to hear.

EUGENIA
Then know.   **SYAVEDRA** [within]

ALVAREZ
What noise is that?

SYAVEDRA
If you are noble enemies,   **VITELLI** [within]
Oppress me not with odds, but kill me fairly.

VITELLI
Stand off, I am too many of my self.

[Enter **BOBADILLA**.

BOBADILLA
Murther, murther, murther, your friend my Lord, Don Sayavedra is set upon in the streets, by your enemies Vitelli, and his Faction: I am almost kill'd with looking on them.

ALVAREZ
I'll free him, or fall with him: draw thy sword
And follow me.

CLARA
Fortune, I give thee thanks
For this occasion once more to use it.

[Exit.

BOBADILLA
Nay, hold not me Madam; if I do any hurt, hurt me.

LUCIO
Oh I am dead with fear! let's flie into
Your Closet, Mother.

EUGENIA
No hour of my life
Secure of danger? heav'n be merciful,
Or now at once dispach me.

[Enter **VITELLI**, pursued by **ALVAREZ** and **SYAVEDRA**, **CLARA** beating of **ANASTRO**.

CLARA
Follow him
Leave me to keep these of.

ALVAREZ
Assault my friend
So near my house?

VITELLI
Nor in it will spare thee,
Though 'twere a Temple: and I'll make it one,
I being the Priest, and thou the sacrifice,
I'll offer to my Uncle.

ALVAREZ
Haste thou to him,
And say I sent thee:

CLARA
'Twas put bravely by,
And that: and yet comes on, and boldly rare,
In the wars, where emulation and example
Joyn to increase the courage, and make less
The danger; valour, and true resolution
Never appear'd so lovely, brave again:
Sure he is more than man, and if he fall;
The best of virtue, fortitude would dye with him:

And can I suffer it? forgive me duty,
So I love valour, as I will protect it
Against my Father, and redeem it, though
'Tis forfeited by one I hate.

VITELLI
Come on,
All is not lost yet: You shall buy me dearer
Before you have me: keep off.

CLARA
Fear me not,
Thy worth has took me prisoner, and my sword
For this time knows thee only for a friend,
And to all else I turn the point of it.

SYAVEDRA
Defend your Fathers enemy?

ALVAREZ
Art thou mad?

CLARA
Are you men rather? shall that valour, which
Begot you lawful honor in the wars,
Prove now the Parent of an infamous Bastard
So foul, yet so long liv'd, as murther will
Be to your shames? have each of you, alone
With your own dangers only, purchas'd glory
From multitudes of enemies, not allowing
Those nearest to you, to have part in it,
And do you now joyn, and lend mutual help
Against a single opposite? hath the mercy
Of the great King, but newly wash'd away
The blood, that with the forfeit of your life
Cleav'd to your name, and family like an ulcer,
In this again to set a deeper dye
Upon your infamy: you'll say he is your foe,
And by his rashness call'd on his own ruin;
Remember yet, he was first wrong'd, and honor
Spurr'd him to what he did, and next the place
Where now he is: your house, which by the laws
Of hospitable duty should protect him;
Have you been twenty years a stranger to it,
To make your entrance now in blood? or think you
Your countrey-man, a true born Spaniard, will be
An offering fit, to please the genius of it?
No, in this I'll presume to teach my Father,

And this first Act of disobedience shall
Confirm I am most dutiful.

ALVAREZ
I am pleas'd
With what I dare not give allowance to;
Unnatural wretch, what wilt thou do?

CLARA
Set free
A noble enemy: come not on, by—
You pass to him, through me: the way is open:
Farewel: when next I meet you, do not look for
A friend, but a vow'd foe; I see you worthy,
And therefore now preserve you, for the honor
Of my sword only:

VITELLI
Were this man a friend,
How would he win me, that being my vow'd foe
Deserves so well? I thank you for my life;
But how I shall deserve it, give me leave
Hereafter to consider.

[Exit.

ALVAREZ
Quit thy fear,
All danger is blown over: I have Letters
To the Governor, in the Kings name, to secure us,
From such attempts hereafter: yet we need not,
That have such strong Guards of our own, dread others;
And to increase thy comfort, know, this young man
Whom with such fervent earnestness you eye,
Is not what he appears, but such a one
As thou with joy wilt bless, thy Daughter Clara.

EUGENIA
A thousand blessings in that word.

ALVAREZ
The reason
Why I have bred her up thus, at more leasure
I will impart unto you, wonder not
At what you have seen her do, it being the least
Of many great and valiant undertakings
She hath made good with honor.

EUGENIA
I'll return
The joy I have in her, with one as great
To you my Alvarez: you, in a man,
Have given to me a Daughter: in a Woman,
I give to you a Son, this was the pledge
You left here with me, whom I have brought up
Different from what he was, as you did Clara,
And with the like success; as she appears
Alter'd by custom, more than Woman, he
Transform'd by his soft life, is less than man.

ALVAREZ
Fortune, in this gives ample satisfaction
For all our sorrows past.

LUCIO
My dearest Sister.

CLARA
Kind Brother.

ALVAREZ
Now our mutual care must be
Imploy'd to help wrong'd nature, to recover
Her right in either of them, lost by custom:
To you I give my Clara, and receive
My Lucio to my charge: and we'll contend
With loving industry, who soonest can
Turn this man woman, or this woman man.

[Exeunt.

ACTUS SECUNDUS

SCÆNA PRIMA

Enter **PACHIECO** and **LAZARILLO**.

PACHIECO
Boy: my Cloak, and Rapier; it fits not a Gentleman of my rank, to walk the streets in Querpo.

LAZARILLO
Nay, you are a very rank Gent. Signior, I am very hungry, they tell me in Sevil here, I look like an Eel, with a mans head: and your neighbor the Smith here hard by, would have borrowed me th' other day, to have fish'd with me, because he had lost his Angle-rod.

PACHIECO

Oh happy thou Lazarillo (being the cause of other mens wits) as in thine own: live lean, and witty still: oppress not thy stomach too much: gross feeders, great sleepers: great sleepers, fat bodies; fat bodies, lean brains: No Lazarillo, I will make thee immortal, change thy Humanity into Deity, for I will teach thee to live upon nothing.

LAZARILLO

Faith Signior, I am immortal then already, or very near it, for I do live upon little or nothing: belike that's the reason the Poets are said to be immortal, for some of them live upon their wits, which is indeed as good as little or nothing: But good Master, let me be mortal still, and let's go to supper.

PACHIECO

Be abstinent; shew not the corruption of thy generation: he that feeds, shall die, therefore, he that feeds not shall live.

LAZARILLO

I; but how long shall he live? there's the question.

PACHIECO

As long as he can without feeding: did'st thou read of the miraculous Maid in Flanders?

LAZARILLO

No, nor of any Maid else; for the miracle of Virginity now-a-days ceases, e'r the Virgin can read Virginity?

PACHIECO

She that liv'd three years without any other sustenance, than the smell of a Rose.

LAZARILLO

I heard of her Signior, but they say her guts shrunk all into Lute-strings, and her neather-parts cling'd together like a Serpents Tail, so that though she continued a woman still above the girdle, beneath yet she was monster.

PACHIECO

So are most women, believe it.

LAZARILLO

Nay all women Signior, that can live only upon the smell of a Rose.

PACHIECO

No part of the History is fabulous.

LAZARILLO

I think rather no part of the Fable is Historical: but for all this, Sir, my rebellious stomach will not let me be immortal: I will be as immortal, as mortal hunger will suffer: put me to a certain stint Sir, allow me but a red herring a day.

PACHIECO

O' de dios: wouldst thou be gluttonous in thy delicacies?

LAZARILLO
He that eats nothing but a red herring a day, shall ne'r be broil'd for the devil's rasher: a Pilchard, Signior, a Surdiny, an Olive, that I may be a Philosopher first, and immortal after.

PACHIECO
Patience Lazarillo; let contemplation be thy food awhile: I say unto thee, one Pease was a Soldiers Provant a whole day, At the destruction of Jerusalem.

[Enter **METALDIE** and **MENDOZA**.

LAZARILLO
I; and it were any where but at the destruction of a place, I'll be hang'd.

METALDIE
Signior Pachieco Alasto, my most ingenious Cobler of Sevil, the bonos noxios to your Signiorie.

PACHIECO
Signior Metaldi de Forgio, my most famous Smith, and man of Mettle, I return your courtesie ten fold, and do humble my Bonnet beneath the Shooe-sole of your congie: the like to you Signior Mendoza Pediculo de Vermim, my most exquisite Hose-heeler.

LAZARILLO
Here's a greeting betwixt a Cobler, a Smith, and a Botcher: they all belong to the foot, which makes them stand so much upon their Gentrie.

MENDOZA
Signior Lazarillo.

LAZARILLO
Ah Signior see: nay, we are all Signiors here in Spain, from the Jakes-farmer to the Grandee, or Adelantado: this Botcher looks as if he were Dough-bak'd, a little Butter now, and I could eat him like an Oaten-cake: his fathers diet was new Cheese and Onions when he got him: what a scallion-fac'd rascal 'tis!

METALDIE
But why Signior Pachieco, do you stand so much on the priority, and antiquity of your quality (as you call it) in comparison of ours?

MENDOZA
I; your reason for that.

PACHIECO
Why thou Iron-pated Smith: and thou Woollen-witted Hose-heeler: hear what I will speak indifferently (and according to antient Writers) of our three professions: and let the upright Lazarillo be both judge and moderator.

LAZARILLO
Still am I the most immortally hungry; that may be.

PACHIECO
Suppose thou wilt derive thy Pedigree, like some of the old Heroes, (as Hercules, Æneas, Achilles) lineally from the gods, making Saturn thy great Grandfather, and Vulcan thy Father: Vulcan was a god.

LAZARILLO
He'll make Vulcan your godfather by and by.

PACHIECO
Yet I say, Saturn was a crabbed block-head, and Vulcan a limping Horn-head, for Venus his wife was a strumpet, and Mars begot all her Children; therefore however, thy original must of necessity spring from Bastardie: further, what can be a more deject spirit in man, than to lay his hands under every ones horses feet, to do him service, as thou dost? For thee, I will be brief, thou dost botch, and not mend, thou art a hider of enormities, viz., Scabs, chilblains, and kib'd heels: much prone thou art to Sects, and Heresies, disturbing State, and Government; for how canst thou be a sound member in the common-wealth, that art so subject to stitches in the ankles? blush, and be silent then, oh ye Mechanicks, compare no more with the politick Cobler: For Coblers (in old time) have prophesied, what may they do now then, that have every day waxed better, and better? have we not the length of every mans foot? are we not daily menders? yea, and what menders? Not horse-menders.

LAZARILLO
Nor manners-menders.

PACHIECO
But soul-menders: Oh divine Coblers; do we not, like the wise man, spin out our own threads, (or our wives for us?) do we not by our sowing the Hide, reap the Beef? are not we of the Gentle-craft, whilst both you are but Crafts-men; You will say, you fear neither Iron nor Steel, and what you get is wrought out of the fire; I must answer you again, though, all this is but forgery: You may likewise say, a man's a man, that has but a hose on his head: I must likewise answer, that man is a botcher, that has a heel'd hose on his head: to conclude, there can be no comparison with the Cobler, who is all in all in the Common-wealth, has his politique eye and ends on every mans steps that walks, and whose course shall be lasting to the worlds end.

METALDIE
I give place: the wit of man is wonderful: thou hast hit the nail on the head, and I will give thee six pots for't, though I ne'r clinch shooe again.

[Enter **VITELLI** and **ALGUAZIER**.

PACHIECO
Who's this? oh our Alguazier: as arrant a knave as e'er wore one head under two offices: he is one side Alguazier.

METALDIE
The other side Serjeant.

MENDOZA
That's both sides carrion I am sure.

PACHIECO
This is he apprehends whores in the way of justice, and lodges 'em in his own house, in the way of profit: he with him, is the Grand Don Vitelli, 'twixt whom and Fernando Alvarez, the mortal hatred is; he is indeed my Don's Bawd, and does at this present, lodge a famous Curtizan of his, lately come from Madrid.

VITELLI
Let her want nothing Signior, she can aske:
What loss or injury you may sustain
I will repair, and recompence your love:
Only that fellows coming I mislike,
And did fore-warn her of him: bear her this
With my best love, at night I'll visit her.

ALGUAZIER
I rest your Lordships Servant.

VITELLI
Good ev'n, Signiors:
Oh Alvarez, thou hast brought a Son with thee
Both brightens, and obscures our Nation,
Whose pure strong beams on us, shoot like the Suns
On baser fires: I would to heaven my bloud
Had never stain'd thy bold unfortunate hand,
That with mine honor I might emulate,
Not persecute such virtue: I will see him,
Though with the hazard of my life: no rest
In my contentious spirits, can I find
Till I have gratify'd him in like kind.

[Exit.

ALGUAZIER
I know you not: what are ye? hence ye base Besegnios.

PACHIECO
Mary Catzo Signior Alguazier, d'ye not know us? why, we are your honest neighbors, the Cobler, Smith, and Botcher, that have so often sate snoaring cheek by joll with your Signiorie, in rug at midnight.

LAZARILLO
Nay, good Signior, be not angry: you must understand, a
Cat, and such an Officer see best in the dark.

METALDIE
By this hand, I could find in my heart to shooe his head.

PACHIECO

Why then know you, Signior; thou mongril, begot at midnight, at the Goal gate, by a Beadle, on a Catchpoles wife, are not you he that was whipt out of Toledo for perjury.

MENDOZA

Next; condemn'd to the Gallies for pilfery, to the Buls pizel.

METALDIE

And after call'd to the Inquisition, for Apostacie.

PACHIECO

Are not you he that rather than you durst goe an industrious voyage being press'd to the Islands, skulk'd till the Fleet was gone, and then earn'd your Royal a day by squiring puncks, and puncklings up and down the City?

LAZARILLO

Are not you a Portuguize born, descended o' the Moors, and came hither into Sevil with your Master, an arrant Tailor, in your red Bonnet, and your blue Jacket, lousie, though now your block-head be cover'd with the Spanish block, and your lashed Shoulders with a Velvet Pee.

PACHIECO

Are not you he that have been of thirty callings, yet ne'r a one lawful? that being a Chandler first, profess'd sincerity, and would sell no man Mustard to his Beef on the Sabbath, and yet sold Hypocrisie all your life time?

METALDIE

Are not you he, that were since a Surgeon to the Stews, and undertook to cure what the Church it self could not, Strumpets that rise to your office by being a great Don's Bawd?

LAZARILLO

That commit men nightly, offenceless, for the gain of a groat a prisoner, which your Beadle seems to put up, when you share three pence?

MENDOZA

Are not you he that is a kisser of men, in drunkenness, and a betrayer in sobriety?

ALGUAZIER

Diabolo: they'll rail me into the Gallies again.

PACHIECO

Yes Signior, thou art even he we speak of all this while: thou mayst by thy place now, lay us by the heels: 'tis true: but take heed, be wiser, pluck not ruin on thine own head: for never was there such an Anatomie, as we shall make thee then: be wise therefore, Oh thou child of the night! Be friends, and shake hands, thou art a proper man, if thy beard were redder: remember thy worshipful function, a Constable; though thou turn'st day into night, and night into day, what of that? watch less and pray more: gird thy beares skin (viz. thy Rug-gowne) to thy loynes, take thy staffe in thy hand, and goe forth at midnight: Let not thy mittens abate the talons of thy authority, but gripe theft and whoredom, wheresoever thou meet'st 'em: bear 'em away like a tempest, and lodge 'em safely in thine own house:

LAZARILLO
Would you have whores and thieves lodgd in such a house?

PACHIECO
They ever do so: I have found a thief, or a whore there, when the whole Suburbs could not furnish me.

LAZARILLO
But why do they lodge there?

PACHIECO
That they may be safe and forth-coming: for in the morning usually, the thief is sent to the Goal, and the whore prostrates her self to the Justice.

MENDOZA
Admirable Pachiecho.

METALDIE
Thou Cobler of Christendom.

ALGUAZIER
There is no railing with these rogues: I will close with 'em, till I can cry quittance: why Signiors, and my honest neighbors, will you impute that as a neglect of my friends, which is an imperfection in me? I have been Sandblind from my infancy: to make you amends you shall sup with me.

LAZARILLO
Shall we sup with ye, Sir? O' my conscience, they have wrong'd the Gentleman extreamly.

ALGUAZIER
And after supper, I have a project to employ you in, shall make you drink and eat merrily this month: I am a little knavish: why, and doe not I know all you to be knaves?

PACHIECO
I grant you, we are all knaves, and will be your knaves:
But oh, while you live, take heed of being a proud knave.

ALGUAZIER
On then pass: I will bear out my staffe, and my staffe shall bear out me.

LAZARILLO
Oh Lazarillo, thou art going to supper.

[Exeunt.

SCÆNA SECUNDA

Enter **LUCIO** and **BOBADILLA**.

LUCIO
Pray be not angry.

BOBADILLA
I am angry, and I will be angry Diabolo: what should you do in the Kitchin, cannot the Cooks lick their fingers without your overseeing? nor the maids make pottage, except your dogs-head be in the pot? Don Lucio, Don Quot-Quean, Don Spinster, wear a Petticoat still, and put on your Smock a' Monday: I will have a baby o' clouts made for it, like a great girl: nay, if you will needs be starching of Ruffs, and sowing of Black-work, I will of a mild, and loving Tutor, become a Tyrant, your Father has committed you to my charge, and I will make a man or a mouse on you.

LUCIO
What would you have me do? this scurvy sword
So galls my thigh: I would 't were burnt: pish, look,
This Cloak will ne'r keep on: these Boots too hide-bound,
Make me walk stiff, as if my legs were frozen,
And my Spurs gingle like a Morris-dancer:
Lord, how my head akes with this roguish Hat;
This masculine attire is most uneasie,
I am bound up in it: I had rather walk
In folio, again, loose like a woman.

BOBADILLA
In Foolio, had you not?
Thou mock to heav'n, and nature, and thy Parents,
Thou tender Leg of Lamb; oh, how he walks
As if he had bepiss'd himself, and fleers!
Is this a gate for the young Cavalier,
Don Lucio, Son and Heir to Alvarez?
Has it a corn? or do's it walk on conscience,
It treads so gingerly? Come on your ways,
Suppose me now your Fathers foe, Vitelli,
And spying you i' th' street, thus I advance
I twist my Beard, and then I draw my sword.

LUCIO
Alas.

BOBADILLA
And thus accost thee: traiterous brat,
How durst thou thus confront me? impious twig
Of that old stock, dew'd with my kinsmans gore,
Draw, for I'll quarter thee in pieces four.

LUCIO

Nay, prethee Bobadilla, leave thy fooling,
Put up thy sword, I will not meddle with ye;
I, justle me, I care not: I'll not draw,
Pray be a quiet man.

BOBADILLA

D'ye hear: answer me, as you would do Don Vitelli, or I'll be so bold as to lay the pomel of my sword
over the hilts of your head: my name's Vitelli, and I'll have the wall.

LUCIO

Why then I'll have the kennel: what a coil you keep!
Signior, what happen'd 'twixt my Sire and your
Kinsman, was long before I saw the world,
No fault of mine, nor will I justifie
My Fathers crimes: forget Sir, and forgive.
'Tis Christianity: I pray put up your sword,
I'll give you any satisfaction
That may become a Gentleman: however
I hope you are bred to more humanity
Than to revenge my Fathers wrong on me
That crave your love, and peace: law-you-now Zancho
Would not this quiet him, were he ten Vitellies.

BOBADILLA

Oh craven-chicken of a Cock o' th' game: well, what remedy? did thy Father see this, O' my conscience,
he would cut off thy Masculine gender, crop thine ears, beat out thine eyes, and set thee in one of the
Pear trees for a scare-crow: As I am Vitelli, I am satisfied; But as I am Bobadilla, Spindola, Zancho,
Steward of the house, and thy Fathers Servant, I could find in my heart to lop off the hinder part of thy
face, or to beat all thy teeth into thy mouth: Oh thou whay-blooded milk-sop, I'll wait upon thee no
longer, thou shalt ev'n wait upon me: come your ways Sir, I shall take a little pains with ye else.

[Enter **CLARA**.

CLARA

Where art thou brother Lucio? ran tan tan ta ran tan ran tan tan ta, ta ran tan tan tan. Oh, I shall no
more see those golden daies, these clothes will never fadge with me: a—O' this filthy vardingale, this
hip-hape: brother, why are womens hanches only limited, confin'd, hoop'd in, as it were with these
same scurvy vardingales?

BOBADILLA

Because womens hanches only are most subject to display and flie out.

CLARA

Bobadilla, rogue, ten Duckets, I hit the prepuce of thy Codpiece.

LUCIO

Hold, if you love my life, Sister: I am not Zancho Bobadilla, I am your brother Lucio: what a fright you have put me in!

CLARA
Brother? and wherefore thus?

LUCIO
Why, Master Steward here, Signior Zancho made me change: he does nothing but mis-use me, and call me Coward, and swears I shall wait upon him.

BOBADILLA
Well: I do no more than I have authority for: would I were away though: for she's as much too manish, as he too womanish: I dare not meddle with her, yet I must set a good face on't (if I had it) I have like charge of you Madam, I am as well to mollifie you, as to quallifie him: what have you to do with Armors, and Pistols, and Javelins, and swords, and such tools? remember Mistriss; nature hath given you a sheath only, to signifie women are to put up mens weapons, not to draw them: look you now, is this a fit trot for a Gentlewoman? You shall see the Court-Ladies move like Goddesses, as if they trode air; they will swim you their measures, like Whiting-mops, as if their feet were finns, and the hinges of their knees oil'd: doe they love to ride great horses, as you do? no, they love to ride great asses sooner: faith, I know not what to say t' ye both: Custom hath turn'd nature topsie-turvie in you.

CLARA
Nay, but Master Steward.

BOBADILLA
You cannot trot so fast, but he ambles as slowly.

CLARA
Signior Spindle, will you hear me?

BOBADILLA
He that shall come to bestride your Virginity, had better be afoot o'er the Dragon.

CLARA
Very well.

BOBADILLA
Did ever Spanish Lady pace so?

CLARA
Hold these a little.

LUCIO
I'll not touch 'em, I.

CLARA
First doe I break your Office o're your pate,
You Dog-skin-fac'd rogue, pilcher, you poor John,

Which I will beat to Stock-fish.

LUCIO
Sister.

BOBADILLA
Madam.

CLARA
You Cittern-head, who have you talk'd to, ha? You nasty, stinking, and ill-countenanc'd Cur.

BOBADILLA
By this hand, I'll bang your brother for this, when I get him alone.

CLARA
How? kick him Lucio, he shall kick you Bob,
Spight o' the nose, that's flat: kick him, I say,
Or I will cut thy head off.

BOBADILLA
Softly y' had best.

CLARA
Now, thou lean, dry'd, and ominous visag'd knave,
Thou false and peremptory Steward, pray,
For I will hang thee up in thine own chain.

LUCIO
Good Sister do not choak him.

BOBADILLA
Murder, murder.

[Exit.

CLARA
Well: I shall meet with ye: Lucio, who bought this?
'Tis a reasonable good one; but there hangs one
Spain's Champion ne'er us'd truer: with this Staffe
Old Alvarez has led up men so close,
They could almost spit in the Cannons mouth,
Whilst I with that, and this well mounted, scour'd
A Horse-troop through, and through, like swift desire,
And seen poor rogues retire, all gore, and gash'd
Like bleeding Shads.

LUCIO
Bless us, Sister Clara.

How desperately you talk: what d' ye call
This Gun a dag?

CLARA
I'll give't thee: a French petronel:
You never saw my Barbary, the Infanta
Bestow'd upon me, as yet Lucio?
Walk down, and see it.

LUCIO
What into the Stable?
Not I, the Jades will kick: the poor Groom there
Was almost spoil'd the other day.

CLARA
Fie on thee,
Thou wilt scarce be a man before thy Mother.

LUCIO
When will you be a woman?

[Enter **ALVAREZ** and **BOBADILLA**.

CLARA
Would I were none.
But natures privy Seal assures me one.

ALVAREZ
Thou anger'st me: can strong habitual custome
Work with such Magick on the mind and manners,
In spight of sex and nature? find out sirrah,
Some skilful fighter.

BOBADILLA
Yes Sir.

ALVAREZ
I will rectifie,
And redeem eithers proper inclination,
Or bray 'em in a morter, and new mold 'em.

[Exit.

BOBADILLA
Believe your eyes, Sir, I tell you, we wash an Ethiop.

CLARA
I strike it for ten Duckets.

ALVAREZ
How now Clara,
Your Breeches on still? and your petticoat
Not yet off Lucio? art thou not guelt?
Or did the cold Muscovite beget thee,
That lay here Lieger in the last great frost?
Art not thou Clara, turn'd a man indeed
Beneath the girdle? and a woman thou?
I'll have you search'd by — I strongly doubt;
We must have these things mended: come goe in.

[Exit.

[Enter **VITELLI** and **BOBADILLA**.

BOBADILLA
With Lucio say you? there is for you.

VITELLI
And there is for thee.

BOBADILLA
I thank you: you have now bought a little advice
Of me; if you chance to have conference with that
Lady there, be very civil, or look to your head: she has
Ten nails, and you have but two eies: If any foolish
Hot motions should chance to rise in the Horizon
Under your equinoctial there, qualifie it as well as
You can, for I fear the elevation of your pole will
Not agree with the Horoscope of her constitution:
She is Bell the Dragon I assure you.

[Exit.

VITELLI
Are you the Lucio, Sir, that sav'd Vitelli?

LUCIO
Not I indeed, Sir, I did never brable;
There walks that Lucio Metamorphosed.

[Exit.

VITELLI
Do ye mock me?

CLARA

No, he does not: I am that
Supposed Lucio that was, but Clara,
That is, and daughter unto Alvarez.

VITELLI

Amazement daunts me; would my life were riddles,
So you were still my fair Expositor:
Protected by a Lady from my death.
Oh, I shall wear an everlasting blush
Upon my cheek from this discovery:
Oh, you the fairest Soldier, I e'er saw;
Each of whose eyes, like a bright beamy Shield,
Conquers without blows, the contentious.

CLARA

Sir, guard your self, you are in your enemies house,
And may be injur'd.

VITELLI

'Tis impossible:
Foe, nor oppressing odds dares prove Vitelli,
If Clara side him, and will call him friend;
I would the difference of our bloods were such
As might with any shift be wip'd away:
Or would to heaven your self were all your name;
That having lost blood by you, I might hope
To raise blood from you. But my black-wing'd fate
Hovers aversely over that fond hope:
And he, whose tongue thus gratifies the daughter,
And Sister of his enemy, wears a sword
To rip the Father and the Brother up.
Thus you that sav'd this wretched life of mine,
Have sav'd it to the ruin of your friends.
That my affections should promiscuously
Dart love and hate at once, both worthily?
Pray let me kiss your hand.

CLARA

You are treacherous,
And come to do me mischief.

VITELLI

Speak on still:
Your words are falser (fair) than my intents,
And each sweet accent far more treacherous; for
Though you speak ill of me, you speak so well,
I doe desire to hear you.

CLARA
Pray be gone:
Or kill me if you please.

VITELLI
Oh, neither can I,
For to be gone, were to destroy my life;
And to kill you, were to destroy my soul:
I am in love, yet must not be in love:
I'll get away apace: yet valiant Lady,
Such gratitude to honor I do owe,
And such obedience to your memory,
That if you will bestow something, that I
May wear about me, it shall bind all wrath,
My most inveterate wrath, from all attempts,
Till you and I meet next.

CLARA
A favour, Sir?
Why, I will give ye good counsel.

VITELLI
That already,
You have bestowed; a Ribbon, or a Glove.

CLARA
Nay, those are tokens for a waiting-maid
To trim the Butler with.

VITELLI
Your feather.

CLARA
Fie; the wenches give them to their serving-men.

VITELLI
That little Ring.

CLARA
'Twill hold you but by th' finger;
And I would have you faster.

VITELLI
Any thing
That I may wear, and but remember you.

CLARA
This smile: my good opinion, or my self.

But that it seems you like not.

VITELLI
Yes, so well:
When any smiles, I will remember yours;
Your good opinion shall in weight poize me
Against a thousand ill: Lastly, your self,
My curious eye now figures in my heart,
Where I will wear you, till the Table break.
So, whitest Angels guard you.

CLARA
Stay Sir, I
Have fitly thought to give, what you as fitly
May not disdain to wear.

VITELLI
What's that?

CLARA
This Sword.
I never heard a man speak till this hour.
His words are golden chains, and now I fear
The Lyonesse hath met a tamer here:
Fie, how his tongue chimes: what was I saying?
Oh: this favour I bequeath you, which I tie
In a Love-knot, fast, ne'er to hurt my friends;
Yet be it fortunate 'gainst all your foes
(For I have neither friend, nor foe, but yours)
As e'er it was to me: I've kept it long,
And value it, next my Virginity:
But good, return it, for I now remember
I vow'd, who purchas'd it, should have me too.

VITELLI
Would that were possible: but alas it is not;
Yet this assure your self, most honour'd Clara,
I'll not infringe a particle of breath
My vow hath offered to ye: nor from this part
Whilst it hath edge, or point, or I a heart.

[Exit.

CLARA
Oh, leave me living: what new exercise
Is crept into my breast, that blauncheth clean
My former nature? I begin to find
I am a woman, and must learn to fight

A softer sweeter battel, than with swords.
I am sick methinks, but the disease I feel
Pleaseth, and punisheth: I warrant love
Is very like this, that folks talke of so;
I skill not what it is, yet sure even here,
Even in my heart, I sensibly perceive
It glows, and riseth like a glimmering flame,
But know not yet the Essence on't, nor name.

[Exit.

ACTUS TERTIUS

SCÆNA PRIMA

Enter **MALRODA** and **ALGUAZIER**.

MALRODA
He must not? nor he shall not, who shall lett him?
You politique Diego, with your face of wisdom;
Don-blirt, the — on your Aphorismes,
Your grave, and Sage-Ale Physiognomy:
Do not I know thee for the Alguazier,
Whose dunghil all the Parish Scavengers
Could never rid? thou Comedy to men,
Whose serious folly is a Butt for all
To shoot their wits at; whilst thou hast not wit,
Nor heart, to answer, or be angry.

ALGUAZIER
Lady.

MALRODA
Peace, peace, you rotten Rogue, supported by
A staffe of rottener office: dare you check
Any accesses that I will allow?
Piorato is my friend, and visits me
In lawful sort to espouse me as his wife;
And who will cross, or shall our enter-views?
You know me sirrah, for no Chambermaid,
That cast her belly, and her wastecoat lately;
Thou think'st thy Constableship is much: not so,
I am ten offices to thee: I, thy house,
Thy house, and office is maintain'd by me.

ALGUAZIER

My house-of-office is maintain'd i' th' garden:
Go too, I know you, and I have contriv'd;
Y'are a delinquent, but I have contriv'd
A poison, though not in the third degree:
I can say, black's your eye, though it be grey;
I have conniv'd at this, your friend, and you:
But what is got by this connivency?
I like his feather well: a proper man,
Of good discourse, fine conversation,
Valiant, and a great carrier of the business,
Sweet breasted, as the Nightingale, or Thrush:
Yet I must tell you; you forget your self,
My Lord Vitellies love, and maintenance
Deserves no other Jack i' th' box, but he:
What though he gather'd first the golden fruit,
And blew your pig's-coat up into a blister,
When you did wait at Court upon his mother;
Has he not well provided for the barn?
Beside, what profit reap I by the other?
If you will have me serve your pleasure, Lady,
Your pleasure must accommodate my service;
As good be virtuous and poor, as not
Thrive by my knavery, all the world would be
Good, prosper'd goodness like to villany.
I am the Kings Vice-gerent by my place;
His right Lieutenant in mine own precinct.

MALRODA
Thou art a right rascal in all mens precincts;
Yet now my pair of twins, of fool, and knave,
Look we are friends; there's Gold for thee, admit
Whom I will have, and keep it from my Don;
And I will make thee richer than thou'rt wise:
Thou shalt be my Bawd, and my Officer:
Thy children shall eat still, my good night Owl,
And thy old wife sell Andirons to the Court,
Be countenanced by the Dons, and wear a hood,
Nay, keep my Garden-house; I'll call her Mother,
Thee Father, my good poysonous Red-hair'd Dill,
And Gold shall daily be thy Sacrifice,
Wrought from a fertile Island of mine own,
Which I will offer, like an Indian Queen.

ALGUAZIER
And I will be thy devil, thou my flesh,
With which I'll catch the world.

MALRODA

Fill some Tobacco,
And bring it in: if Piorato come
Before my Don, admit him; if my Don
Before my Love, conduct him, my dear Devil.

[Exit.

ALGUAZIER
I will my dear Flesh: first come, first serv'd. Well said.
Oh equal Heaven, how wisely thou disposest
Thy several gifts! one's born a great rich fool,
For the subordinate knave to work upon:
Anothers poor, with wits addition,
Which well or ill-us'd, builds a living up;
And that too from the Sire oft descends:
Only fair virtue, by traduction
Never succeeds, and seldom meets success,
What have I then to do with't? My free will
Left me by heaven, makes me or good, or ill:
Now since vice gets more in this vicious world
Than Piety, and my Stars confluence
Enforce my disposition to affect
Gain, and the name of rich, let who will practise
War, and grow that way great: religious,
And that way good: my chief felicity
Is wealth the nurse of sensuality:
And he that mainly labours to be rich,
Must scratch great scabs, and claw a Strumpets itch.

[Exit.

SCÆNA SECUNDA

Enter **PIORATO** and **BOBADILLA** with Letters.

PIORATO
To say, Sir, I will wait upon your Lord,
Were not to understand my self.

BOBADILLA
To say Sir,
You will do any thing but wait upon him,
Were not to understand my Lord.

PIORATO
I'll meet him

Some half hour hence, and doubt not but to render
His Son a man again: the cure is easie,
I have done divers.

BOBADILLA
Women do ye mean, Sir?

PIORATO
Cures I do mean, Sir: be there but one spark
Of fire remaining in him unextinct,
With my discourse I'll blow it to a flame;
And with my practice into action:
I have had one so full of childish fear,
And womanish-hearted sent to my advice,
He durst not draw a knife to cut his meat.

BOBADILLA
And how Sir, did you help him?

PIORATO
Sir, I kept him
Seven daies in a dark room by a Candle-light,
A plenteous Table spread with all good meats,
Before his eyes, a Case of keen broad Knives,
Upon the board, and he so watch'd he might not
Touch the least modicum, unless he cut it:
And thus I brought him first to draw a knife.

BOBADILLA
Good.

PIORATO
Then for ten daies did I diet him
Only with burnt Pork, Sir, and gammons of Bacon;
A pill of Caveary now and then,
Which breeds choler adust you know.

BOBADILLA
'Tis true.

PIORATO
And to purge phlegmatick humor, and cold crudities;
In all that time he drank me Aqua-fortis,
And nothing else but—

BOBADILLA
Aqua-vitæ Signior,
For Aqua-fortis poisons.

PIORATO
Aqua-fortis
I say again: what's one man's poison, Signior,
Is anothers meat or drink.

BOBADILLA
Your patience, Sir;
By your good patience, h' had a huge cold stomach.

PIORATO
I fir'd it: and gave him then three sweats
In the Artillery-yard three drilling daies:
And now he'll shoot a Gun, and draw a Sword,
And fight with any man in Christendom.

BOBADILLA
A receipt for a coward: I'll be bold, Sir,
To write your good prescription.

PIORATO
Sir, hereafter
You shall, and underneath it put probatum:
Is your chain right?

BOBADILLA
'Tis both right and just Sir;
For though I am a Steward, I did get it
With no mans wrong.

PIORATO
You are witty.

BOBADILLA
So, so.
Could you not cure one Sir, of being too rash
And over-daring? there now's my disease:
Fool-hardy as they say, for that in sooth,
I am.

PIORATO
Most easily.

BOBADILLA
How?

PIORATO
To make you drunk, Sir,

With small Beer once a day, and beat you twice,
Till you be bruis'd all over: if that help not,
Knock out your brains.

BOBADILLA
This is strong Physick Signior,
And never will agree with my weak body:
I find the medicine worse than the malady,
And therefore will remain fool-hardy still:
You'll come, Sir?

PIORATO
As I am a Gentleman.

BOBADILLA
A man o' th' Sword should never break his word.

PIORATO
I'll overtake you: I have only, Sir
A complimental visitation
To offer to a Mistriss lodg'd here by.

BOBADILLA
A Gentlewoman?

PIORATO
Yes Sir.

BOBADILLA
Fair, and comely?

PIORATO
Oh Sir, the Paragon, the Non-paril
Of Sevil, the most wealthy Mine of Spain,
For beauty, and perfection.

BOBADILLA
Say you so?
Might not a man entreat a curtesie,
To walk along with you Signior, to peruse
This dainty Mine, though not to dig in't Signior?
Hauh—I hope you'll not denie me, being a stranger;
Though I am a Steward, I am flesh and blood,
And frail as other men.

PIORATO
Sir, blow your nose:
I dare not for the world: no, she is kept

By a great Don, Vitelli.

BOBADILLA
How?

PIORATO
'Tis true.

BOBADILLA
See, things will veer about: this Don Vitelli
Am I to seek now, to deliver Letters
From my young Mistriss Clara: and I tell you,
Under the Rose, because you are a stranger,
And my special friend, I doubt there is
A little foolish love betwixt the parties,
Unknown unto my Lord.

PIORATO
Happy discovery:
My fruit begins to ripen: hark you Sir,
I would not wish you now, to give those Letters:
But home, and ope this to Madona Clara,
Which when I come I'll justifie, and relate
More amply, and particularly.

BOBADILLA
I approve
Your counsel, and will practise it: bazilos manos:
Here's two chewres chewr'd: when wisdom is imploy'd
'Tis ever thus: your more acquaintance, Signior:
I say not better, least you think, I thought not
Yours good enough.

[Exit.

[Enter **ALGUAZIER**.

PIORATO
Your servant excellent Steward.
Would all the Dons in Spain had no more brains,
Here comes the Alguazier: dieu vous guard Monsieur.
Is my Cuz stirring yet?

ALGUAZIER
Your Cuz (good cosin?)
A whore is like a fool, a kin to all
The gallants in the Town: Your Cuz, good Signior,
Is gone abroad; Sir, with her other Cosin,

My Lord Vitelli: since when there hath been
Some dozen Cosins here to enquire for her.

PIORATO
She's greatly ally'd Sir.

ALGUAZIER
Marry is she, Sir,
Come of a lusty kindred: the truth is,
I must connive no more: no more admittance
Must I consent to; my good Lord has threatned me,
And you must pardon.

PIORATO
Out upon thee man,
Turn honest in thine age? one foot i'th' grave?
Thou shalt not wrong thy self so, for a million:
Look, thou three-headed Cerberus (for wit
I mean) here is one sop, and two, and three,
For every chop a bit.

ALGUAZIER
I marry Sir:
Well, the poor heart loves you but too well.
We have been talking on you 'faith this hour:
Where, what I said, goe too: she loves your valour;
Oh, and your Musick most abominably:
She is within Sir, and alone: what mean you?

PIORATO
That is your Sergeants side, I take it Sir;
Now I endure your Constables much better;
There is less danger in't: for one you know
Is a tame harmless monster in the light,
The Sergeant salvage both by day, and night.

ALGUAZIER
I'll call her to you for that.

PIORATO
No, I will charm her.

[Enter **MALRODA**.

ALGUAZIER
She's come.

PIORATO

My Spirit.

MALRODA
Oh my Sweet,
Leap hearts to lips, and in our kisses meet.

SONG.

PIORATO
Turn, turn thy beauteous face away.
How pale and sickly looks the day,
In emulation of thy brighter beams!
Oh envious light, fli, flie, begone,
Come night, and piece two breasts as one;
When what love does, we will repeat in dreams.
Yet (thy eyes open) who can day hence fright,
Let but their Lids fall, and it will be night.

ALGUAZIER
Well, I will leave you to your fortitude;
And you to temperance: ah, ye pretty pair,
'Twere sin to sunder you. Lovers being alone
Make one of two, and day and night all one.
But fall not out, I charge you, keep the peace;
You know my place else.

[Exit.

MALRODA
No, you will not marry:
You are a Courtier, and can sing (my Love)
And want no Mistrisses: but yet I care not,
I'll love you still; and when I am dead for you,
Then you'll believe my truth.

PIORATO
You kill me (fair)
It is my lesson that you speak: have I
In any circumstance deserv'd this doubt?
I am not like your false and perjur'd Don
That here maintains you, and has vow'd his faith,
And yet attempts in way of marriage
A Lady not far off.

MALRODA
How's that?

PIORATO

'Tis so:
And therefore Mistriss, now the time is come
You may demand his promise; and I swear
To marry you with speed.

MALRODA
And with that Gold
Which Don Vitelli gives, you'll walk some voyage
And leave me to my Trade; and laugh, and brag,
How you o'er-reach'd a whore, and gull'd a Lord.

PIORATO
You anger me extreamly: fare you well.
What should I say to be believ'd? expose me
To any hazard; or like jealous Juno
(Th' incensed step-mother of Hercules)
Design me labours most impossible,
I'll doe 'em, or die in 'em; so at last
You will believe me.

MALRODA
Come, we are friends: I do,
I am thine, walk in: my Lord has sent me outsides,
But thou shall have 'em, the colours are too sad:

PIORATO
'Faith Mistriss, I want clothes indeed.

MALRODA
I have
Some Gold too, for my servant.

PIORATO
And I have
A better mettal for my Mistriss.

[Exeunt.

SCÆNA TERTIA

Enter **VITELLI** and **ALGUAZIER**, at several doors.

ALGUAZIER
Undone—wit now or never help me: my Master
He will cut my throat, I am a dead Constable;
And he'll not be hang'd neither, there's the grief:

The party, Sir, is here.

VITELLI
What?

ALGUAZIER
He was here;
I cry your Lordship mercy: but I ratled him;
I told him here was no companions
For such debauch'd, and poor condition'd fellows;
I bid him venture not so desperately
The cropping of his ears, slitting his nose,
Or being gelt.

VITELLI
'Twas well done.

ALGUAZIER
Please your honor,
I told him there were Stews, and then at last
Swore three or four great oaths she was remov'd,
Which I did think I might, in conscience,
Being for your Lordship.

VITELLI
What became of him?

ALGUAZIER
Faith Sir, he went away with a flea in's ear,
Like a poor cur, clapping his trundle tail
Betwixt his legs.—A chi ha, a chi ha, a chi ha—now luck.

[Enter **MALRODA** and **PIORATO**.

MALRODA
'Tis he, do as I told thee: Bless thee Signior.
Oh, my dear Lord.

VITELLI
Malroda, what alone?

MALRODA
She never is alone, that is accompanied
With noble thoughts, my Lord; and mine are such,
Being only of your Lordship.

VITELLI
Pretty Lass.

MALRODA
Oh my good Lord, my Picture's done: but 'faith
It is not like; nay, this way Sir, the light
Strikes best upon it here.

PIORATO
Excellent wench.

[Exit.

ALGUAZIER
I am glad the danger's over.

[Exit.

VITELLI
'Tis wondrous like,
But that Art cannot counterfeit what Nature
Could make but once.

MALRODA
All's clear; another tune
You must hear from me now: Vitelli, thou'rt
A most perfidious and a perjur'd man,
As ever did usurp Nobility.

VITELLI
What meanst thou Mal?

MALRODA
Leave your betraying smiles,
And change the tunes of your inticing tongues
To penitential prayers; for I am great
In labour, even with anger, big with child
Of womans rage, bigger than when my womb
Was pregnant by thee: go seducer, flie
Out of the world, let me the last wretch be
Dishonored by thee: touch me not, I loath
My very heart, because thou lay'st there long;
A woman's well help'd up, that's confident
In e'er a glittering outside on you all:
Would I had honestly been match'd to some
Poor Countrey-swain, e'er known the vanity
Of Court: peace then had been my portion,
Nor had been cozen'd by an hours pomp
To be a whore unto my dying day.

VITELLI

Oh the uncomfortable waies such women have,
Their different speech and meaning, no assurance
In what they say or do: Dissemblers
Even in their prayers, as if the weeping Greek
That flatter'd Troy a-fire, had been their Adam;
Lyers, as if their mother had been made
Only of all the falshood of the man,
Dispos'd into that rib: Do I know this,
And more: nay, all that can concern this Sex,
With the true end of my creation?
Can I with rational discourse sometimes
Advance my spirit into Heaven, before
'T has shook hands with my body, and yet blindly
Suffer my filthy flesh to master it,
With sight of such fair frail beguiling objects?
When I am absent, easily I resolve
Ne'er more to entertain those strong desires
That triumph o'er me, even to actual sin;
Yet when I meet again those sorcerers eies,
Their beams my hardest resolutions thaw,
As if that cakes of Ice and July met,
And her sighs powerful as the violent North,
Like a light feather twirl me round about
And leave me in mine own low state again.
What ayl'st thou? prethee weep not: Oh, those tears
If they were true, and rightly spent, would raise
A flow'ry spring i'th' midst of January:
Celestial Ministers with Chrystal cups
Would stoop to save 'em for immortal drink:
But from this passion; why all this?

MALRODA

Do ye ask?
You are marrying: having made me unfit
For any man, you leave me fit for all:
Porters must be my burthens now, to live,
And fitting me your self for Carts, and Beadles,
You leave me to 'em: And who of all the world
But the virago, your great Arch-foes daughter?
But on: I care not, this poor rush: 'twill breed
An excellent Comedy: ha, ha: 't makes me laugh:
I cannot choose: the best is, some report
It is a match for fear, not love o' your side.

VITELLI

Why how the devil knows she, that I saw
This Lady? are all whores, piec'd with some witch?

I will be merry, 'faith 'tis true, sweet heart,
I am to marry?

MALRODA
Are you? you base Lord,
By — I'll pistol thee.

VITELLI
A roaring whore?
Take heed, there's a Correction-house hard by:
You ha' learn'd this o' your swordman, that I warn'd you of,
Your Fencers, and your drunkards: but whereas
You upbraid me with oaths, why I must tell you
I ne'er promis'd you marriage, nor have vow'd,
But said I lov'd you, long as you remain'd
The woman I expected, or you swore,
And how you have fail'd of that (sweet-heart) you know.
You fain would shew your power, but fare you well,
I'll keep no more faith with an infidel.

MALRODA
Nor I my bosome for a Turk: d' ye hear?
Goe, and the devil take me, if ever
I see you more: I was too true.

VITELLI
Come, pish:
That devil take the falsest of us two.

MALRODA
Amen.

VITELLI
You are an ill Clark; and curse your self:
Madness transports you: I confess, I drew you
Unto my Will: but you must know that must not
Make me doat on the habit of my sin.
I will, to settle you to your content,
Be master of my word: and yet he ly'd
That told you I was marrying, but in thought:
But will you slave me to your tyranny
So cruelly I shall not dare to look
Or speak to other women? make me not
Your smock's Monopolie: come, let's be friends:
Look, here's a Jewel for thee: I will come
At night, and—

MALRODA

What 'yfaith: you shall not, Sir.

VITELLI
'Faith, and troth, and verily, but I will.

MALRODA
Half drunk, to make a noise, and rail?

VITELLI
No, no,
Sober, and dieted for the nonce: I am thine,
I have won the day.

MALRODA
The night (though) shall be mine.

[Exeunt.

SCÆNA QUARTA

Enter **CLARA** and **BOBADILLA** with Letters.

CLARA
What said he, sirrah?

BOBADILLA
Little, or nothing: faith I saw him not,
Nor will not: he doth love a strumpet, Mistriss,
Nay, keeps her spitefully, under the Constables nose,
It shall be justified by the Gentleman
Your brothers Master that is now within
A practising: there are your Letters: come
You shall not cast your self away, while I live,
Nor will I venture my Right worshipful place
In such a business—here's your Mother, down:
And he that loves you: another 'gates fellow, I wish,
If you had any grace.

[Enter **EUGENIA** and **SYAVEDRA**.

CLARA
Well rogue.

BOBADILLA
I'll in, to see Don Lucio manage, he'll make
A pretty piece of flesh, I promise you,

He does already handle his weapon finely.

[Exit.

EUGENIA
She knows your love, Sir, and the full allowance
Her Father and my self approve it with,
And I must tell you, I much hope it hath
Wrought some impression by her alteration;
She sighs, and saies, forsooth, and cries heigh-ho,
She'll take ill words o' th' Steward, and the Servants,
Yet answer affably, and modestly:
Things Sir, not usual with her: there she is,
Change some few words.

SYAVEDRA
Madam, I am bound t'ye;
How now, fair Mistriss, working?

CLARA
Yes forsooth,
Learning to live another day.

SYAVEDRA
That needs not.

CLARA
No forsooth: by my truly but it does,
We know not what we may come to.

EUGENIA
'Tis strange.

SYAVEDRA
Come, I ha begg'd leave for you to play.

CLARA
Forsooth
'Tis ill for a fair Lady to be idle.

SYAVEDRA
She had better be well-busied, I know that.
Turtle: me thinks you mourn, shall I sit by you?

CLARA
If you be weary, Sir, you had best be gone
(I work not a true stitch) now you're my mate.

SYAVEDRA

If I be so, I must do more than side you.

CLARA

Ev'n what you will, but tread me.

SYAVEDRA

Shall we bill?

CLARA

Oh no, forsooth.

SYAVEDRA

Being so fair, my Clara,
Why d'ye delight in Black-work?

CLARA

Oh White Sir,
The fairest Ladies like the blackest men:
I ever lov'd the colour: all black things
Are least subject to change.

SYAVEDRA

Why, I do love
A black thing too: and the most beauteous faces
Have oftnest of them: as the blackest eyes,
Jet-arched brows, such hair: I'll kiss your hand.

CLARA

'Twill hinder me my work Sir: and my Mother
Will chide me, if I do not do my taske.

SYAVEDRA

Your Mother, nor your Father shall chide: you
Might have a prettier taske, would you be rul'd,
And look with open eyes.

CLARA

I stare upon you:
And broadly see you, a wondrous proper man,
Yet 'twere a greater taske for me to love you
Than I shall ever work Sir, in seven year,
—O' this stitching, I had rather feel
Two, than sow one:—this rogue h' as given me a stitch good
faith sir: I shall prick you.
Clean cross my heart:

SYAVEDRA

In gooder faith, I would prick you againe.

CLARA
Now you grow troublesome: pish, the man is foolish.

SYAVEDRA
Pray wear these trifles.

CLARA
Neither you, nor trifles,
You are a trifle, wear your self, Sir, out,
And here no more trifle the time away.

SYAVEDRA
Come; you're deceiv'd in me, I will not wake,
Nor fast, nor dye for you.

CLARA
Goose, be not you deceiv'd,
I cannot like, nor love, nor live with you,
Nor fast, nor watch, nor pray for you.

EUGENIA
Her old fit.

SYAVEDRA
Sure this is not the way, nay, I will break
Your melancholly.

CLARA
I shall break your pate then,
Away, you sanguine scabbard.

EUGENIA
Out upon thee
Thou'lt break my heart, I am sure.

[Enter **ALVAREZ**, **PIORATO**, **LUCIO** and **BOBADILLA**.

SYAVEDRA
She's not yet tame.

ALVAREZ
On Sir; put home: or I shall goad you here
With this old Fox of mine, that will bite better:
Oh, the brave age is gone; in my young daies
A Chevalier would stock a needles point
Three times together: strait i' th' hams?

Or shall I give ye new Garters?

BOBADILLA
Faith old Master.
There's little hope: the linnen sure was danck
He was begot in, he's so faint, and cold:

[Two Torches ready.

Ev'n send him to Toledo, there to study,
For he will never fadge with these Toledos;
Bear ye up your point there; pick his teeth: Oh base.

PIORATO
Fie: you are the most untoward Scholar: bear
Your body gracefully: what a posture's there?
You lie too open-breasted.

LUCIO
Oh!

PIORATO
You'ld never
Make a good States-man:

LUCIO
Pray no more.
I hope to breathe in peace, and therefore need not
The practise of these dangerous qualities,
I do not mean to live by't; for I trust
You'll leave me better able.

ALVAREZ
Not a Button:
Let's goe get us a new heir.

EUGENIA
I by my troth: your daughter's as untoward.

ALVAREZ
I will break thee bone by bone, and bake thee,
E'r I'll ha' such a wooden Son to inherit:
Take him a good knock; see how that will work.

PIORATO
Now, for your life Signior:

LUCIO

Oh: alas, I am kill'd
My eye is out: look Father: Zancho:
I'll play the fool no more thus, that I will not.

CLARA
'Heart: ne'r a rogue in Spain shall wrong my brother
Whilst I can hold a sword.

PIORATO
Hold Madam, Madam.

ALVAREZ
Clara.

EUGENIA
Daughter.

BOBADILLA
Mistress.

PIORATO
Bradamante.
Hold, hold I pray.

ALVAREZ
The devil's in her, o'the other side sure,
There's Gold for you: they have chang'd what ye calt's:
Will no cure help? well I have one experiment,
And if that fail, I'll hang him, then here's an end on't.
Come you along with me: and you Sir:

[Exeunt **ALVAREZ, EUGENIA, LUCIO**.

BOBADILLA
Now are you going to drowning.

SYAVEDRA
I'll ev'n along with ye: she's too great a Lady
For me, and would prove more then my match.

[Exit.

CLARA
You'r he spoke of Vitelli to the Stewerd:

PIORATO
Yes, and I thank you, you have beat me for't.

CLARA
But are you sure you do not wrong him?

PIORATO
Sure?
So sure, that if you please venture your self
I'll shew you him, and his Cokatrice together,
And you shall hear 'em talk.

CLARA
Will you? by — Sir
You shall endear me ever: and I ask
You mercy.

PIORATO
You were somewhat boystrous.

CLARA
There's Gold to make you amends: and for this pains,
I'll gratifie you farther: I'll but masque me
And walk along with ye: faith let's make a night on't.

[Exit.

SCÆNA QUINTA

Enter **ALGUAZIER, PACHIECO, MENDOZA, METALDI, LAZARILLO**.

ALGUAZIER
Come on my brave water-Spaniels, you that hunt Ducks in the night: and hide more knavery under your gownes than your betters: observe my precepts, and edifie by my doctrine: at yond corner will I set you; if drunkards molest the street, and fall to brabling, knock you down the malefactors, and take you up their cloaks and hats, and bring them to me: they are lawful prisoners, and must be ransom'd ere they receive liberty: what else you are to execute upon occasion, you sufficiently know, and therefore I abbreviate my Lecture.

METALDIE
We are wise enough, and warm enough.

MENDOZA
Vice this night shall be apprehended.

PACHIECO
The terror of rug-gownes shall be known: and our bils
Discharge us of after recknings.

LAZARILLO
I will do any thing, so I may eat.

PACHIECO
Lazarillo, We will spend no more; now we are grown worse, we will live better: let us follow our calling faithfully.

ALGUAZIER
Away, then the Common-wealth is our Mistress: and who
Would serve a common Mistress, but to gain by her?

[Exeunt.

ACTUS QUARTUS

SCÆNA PRIMA

Enter **VITELLI**, **LAMORAL**, **GENEVORA**, **ANASTRO** and two **PAGES** with lights.

LAMORAL
I pray you see the Masque, my Lord.

ANASTRO
'Tis early night yet.

GENEVORA
O if it be so late, take me along:
I would not give advantage to ill tongues
To tax my being here, without your presence
To be my warrant.

VITELLI
You might spare this, Sister,
Knowing with whom I leave you; one that is
By your allowance, and his choice, your Servant,
And may my councel and perswasion work it,
Your husband speedily: For your entertainment
My thanks; I will not rob you of the means
To do your Mistriss some acceptable service
In waiting on her to my house.

GENEVORA
My Lord.

VITELLI
As you respect me, without farther trouble

Retire, and fast those pleasures prepar'd for you,
And leave me to my own ways.

LAMORAL
When you please Sir.

[Exeunt.

Enter **MALRODA** and **ALGUAZIER**.

MALRODA
You'll leave my Chamber?

ALGUAZIER
Let us but bill once,
My Dove, my Sparrow, and I, with my office
Will be thy slaves for ever.

MALRODA
Are you so hot?

ALGUAZIER
But tast the difference of a man in place,
You'l find that when authority pricks him forward,
Your Don, nor yet your Diego comes not near him
To do a Lady right: no men pay dearer
For their stoln sweets, than we: three minutes trading
Affords to any sinner a protection
For three years after: think on that, I burn;
But one drop of your bounty.

MALRODA
Hence you Rogue,
Am I fit for you? is't not grace sufficient
To have your staff, a bolt to bar the door
Where a Don enters, but that you'l presume
To be his taster?

ALGUAZIER
Is no more respect
Due to this rod of justice?

MALRODA
Do you dispute?

Good Doctor of the Dungeon, not a word more,
—If you do, my Lord Vitelli knows it.

ALGUAZIER
Why I am big enough to answer him,
Or any man.

MALRODA
'Tis well.

VITELLI [within]
Malroda.

ALGUAZIER
How?

MALRODA
You know the voice, and now crowch like a Cur,
Tane worrying sheep: I now could have you guelded
For a Bawd rampant: but on this submission
For once I spare you.

ALGUAZIER
I will be reveng'd—
My honorable Lord.

[Enter **VITELLI**.

VITELLI
There's for thy care.

ALGUAZIER
I am mad, stark mad: proud Pagan scorn her host?
I would I were but valiant enough to kick her,

[Enter **PIORATO** and **CLARA** above.

I'ld wish no manhood else.

MALRODA
What's that?

ALGUAZIER
I am gone.

[Exit.

PIORATO

You see I have kept my word.

CLARA
But in this object
Hardly deserv'd my thanks.

PIORATO
Is there ought else
You will command me?

CLARA
Only your sword
Which I must have: nay willingly I yet know
To force it, and to use it.

PIORATO
'Tis yours Lady.

CLARA
I ask no other guard.

PIORATO
If so I leave you:
And now, if that the Constable keep his word,
A poorer man may chance to gull a Lord.

[Exit.

MALRODA
By this good — you shall not.

VITELLI
By this—
I must, and will, Malroda; What do you make
A stranger of me?

MALRODA
I'll be so to you,
And you shall find it.

VITELLI
These are your old arts
T'endear the game you know I come to hunt for,
Which I have born too coldly.

MALRODA
Do so still,
For if I heat you, hang me.

VITELLI

If you do not
I know who'll starve for't: why, thou shame of women,
Whose folly, or whose impudence is greater
Is doubtful to determine; this to me
That know thee for a whore.

MALRODA

And made me one,
Remember that.

VITELLI

Why should I but grow wise
And tye that bounty up, which nor discretion
Nor honor can give way to; thou wouldst be
A Bawd e're twenty, and within a Month
A barefoot, lowzie, and diseased whore,
And shift thy lodgings oftner than a rogue
That's whipt from post to post.

MALRODA

Pish: all our Colledge
Know you can rail well in this kind.

CLARA

For me
He never spake so well.

VITELLI

I have maintain'd thee
The envy of great fortunes, made thee shine
As if thy name were glorious: stuck thee full
Of jewels, as the firmament of Stars,
And in it made thee so remarkable
That it grew questionable, whether virtue poor,
Or vice so set forth as it is in thee,
Were even by modesties self to be preferr'd,
And am I thus repaid?

MALRODA

You are still my debtor;
Can this (though true) be weigh'd with my lost honor,
Much less my faith? I have liv'd private to you,
And but for you, had ne'r known what lust was,
Nor what the sorrow for't.

VITELLI

'Tis false.

MALRODA
'Tis true,
But how return'd by you, thy whole life being
But one continued act of lust, and Shipwrack
Of womens chastities.

VITELLI
But that I know
That she that dares be damn'd, dares any thing,
I should admire thy tempting me: but presume not
On the power you think you hold o're my affections,
It will deceive you: yield, and presently
Or by the inflamed blood, which thou must quench
I'll make a forcible entry.

MALRODA
Touch me not:
You know I have a throat, — if you do
I will cry out a rape, or sheath this here,
Ere I'll be kept, and us'd for Julip-water
T'allay the heat which lushious meats and wine
And not desire hath rais'd.

VITELLI
A desperate devil,
My blood commands my reason; I must take
Some milder way.

MALRODA
I hope (dear Don) I fit you.
The night is mine, although the day was yours
You are not fasting now: this speeding trick
Which I would as a principle leave to all,
That make their maintenance out of their own Indies,
As I do now; my good old mother taught me,
Daughter, quoth she, contest not with your lover
His stomach being empty; let wine heat him,
And then you may command him: 'tis a sure one:
His looks shew he is coming.

VITELLI
Come this needs not,
Especially to me: you know how dear
I ever have esteemed you.

CLARA

Lost again.

VITELLI
That any sight of yours, hath power to change
My strongest resolution, and one tear
Sufficient to command a pardon from me,
For any wrong from you, which all mankind
Should kneel in vain for.

MALRODA
Pray you pardon those
That need your favor, or desire it.

VITELLI
Prethee.
Be better temper'd: I'll pay as a forfeit
For my rash anger, this purse fil'd with Gold.
Thou shalt have servants, gowns, attires, what not?
Only continue mine.

MALRODA
'Twas this I fish'd for.

VITELLI
Look on me, and receive it.

MALRODA
Well, you know
My gentle nature, and take pride t'abuse it:
You see a trifle pleases me, we are friends;
This kiss, and this confirms it.

CLARA
With my ruine.

MALRODA
I'll have this diamond, and this pearl.

VITELLI
They are yours.

MALRODA
But will you not, when you have what you came for,
Take them from me to morrow? 'tis a fashion
Your Lords of late have us'd.

VITELLI
But I'll not follow.

CLARA
That any man at such a rate as this
Should pay for his repentance.

VITELLI
Shall we to bed now?

MALRODA
Instantly, Sweet; yet now I think on't better
There's something first that in a word or two
I must acquaint you with.

CLARA
Can I cry ay me,
To this against my self? I'll break this match,
Or make it stronger with my blood.

[Descends.

[Enter **ALGUAZIER**, **PIORATO**, **PACHIECO**, **METALDI**, **MENDOZA**, **LAZARILLO** &c.

ALGUAZIER
I am yours.
A Don's not priviledg'd here more than your self,
Win her, and wear her.

PIORATO
Have you a Priest ready?

ALGUAZIER
I have him for thee, Lad; and when I have
Married this scornful whore to this poor gallant,
She will make suit to me; there is a trick
To bring a high-pris'd wench upon her knees:
For you my fine neat Harpyes stretch your tallons
And prove your selves true night-Birds.

PACHIECO
Take my word
For me and all the rest.

LAZARILLO
If there be meat
Or any banquet stirring, you shall see
How I'll bestow my self.

ALGUAZIER

When they are drawn,
Rush in upon 'em: all's fair prize you light on:
I must away: your officer may give way
To the Knavery of his watch, but must not see it.
You all know where to find me.

[Exit.

METALDIE
There look for us.

VITELLI
Who's that?

MALRODA
My Piorato, welcome, welcome:
Faith had you not come when you did my Lord
Had done I know not what to me.

VITELLI
I am gul'd,
First cheated of my Jewels, and then laugh'd at:
Sirha, what makes you here?

PIORATO
A business brings me,
More lawful than your own.

VITELLI
How's that, you slave?

MALRODA
He's such, that would continue her a whore
Whom he would make a wife of.

VITELLI
I'll tread upon
The face you doat on, strumpet.

[Enter **CLARA**.

PACHIECO
Keep the peace there.

VITELLI
A plot upon my life too?

METALDIE

Down with him.

CLARA
Show your old valor, and learn from a woman;
One Eagle has a world of odds against
A flight of Dawes, as these are.

PIORATO
Get you off,
I'll follow instantly.

PACHIECO
Run for more help there.

[Exeunt all but **VITELLI** and **CLARA**.

VITELLI
Loss of my gold, and jewels, and the wench too
Afflicts me not so much, as th'having Clara
The witness of my weakness.

CLARA
He turns from me,
And yet I may urge merit, since his life
Is made my second gift.

VITELLI
May I ne'r prosper
If I know how to thank her.

CLARA
Sir, your pardon
For pressing thus beyond a Virgins bounds
Upon your privacies: and let my being
Like to a man, as you are, be th'excuse
Of my solliciting that from you, which shall not
Be granted on my part, although desir'd
By any other: Sir, you understand me,
And 'twould shew nobly in you, to prevent
From me a farther boldness, which I must
Proceed in, if you prove not merciful,
Though with my loss of blushes and good name.

VITELLI
Madam, I know your will, and would be thankful
If it were possible I could affect
The daughter of an enemy.

CLARA
That fair false one
Whom with fond dotage you have long pursu'd
Had such a father: she to whom you pay
Dearer for your dishonor, than all titles
Ambitious men hunt for, are worth.

VITELLI
'Tis truth.

CLARA
Yet, with her, as a friend you still exchange
Health for diseases, and, to your disgrace,
Nourish the rivals to your present pleasures,
At your own charge, us'd as a property
To give a safe protection to her lust,
Yet share in nothing but the shame of it.

VITELLI
Grant all this so, to take you for a wife
Were greater hazard; for should I offend you
(As 'tis not easy still to please a woman)
You are of so great a spirit, that I must learn
To wear your petticoat, for you will have
My breeches from me.

CLARA
Rather from this hour
I here abjure all actions of a man,
And will esteem it happiness from you
To suffer like a woman: love, true love
Hath made a search within me, and expell'd
All but my natural softness, and made perfect
That which my parents care could not begin.
I will show strength in nothing, but my duty,
And glad desire to please you, and in that
Grow every day more able.

VITELLI
Could this be,
What a brave race might I beget? I find
A kind of yielding; and no reason why
I should hold longer out: she's young, and fair,
And chast; for sure, but with her leave, the Devil
Durst not attempt her: Madam, though you have
A Soldiers arm, your lips appear as if
They were a Ladies.

CLARA
They dare Sir, from you
Endure the tryal.

VITELLI
Ha: once more I pray you:
The best I ever tasted; and 'tis said
I have prov'd many, 'tis not safe I fear
To ask the rest now: well, I will leave whoring
And luck herein send me with her: worthiest Lady,
I'll wait upon you home, and by the way
(If ere I marry, as I'll not forswear it)
Tell you, you are my wife.

CLARA
Which if you do,
From me all man-kind women, learn to woe.

[Exeunt.

SCÆNA TERTIA

Enter **ALGUAZIER, PACHIECO, METALDI, MENDOZA, LAZARILLO.**

ALGUAZIER
A cloak? good purchase, and rich hangers? well,
We'll share ten Pistolets a man.

LAZARILLO
Yet still
I am monstrous hungry: could you not deduct
So much out of the gross sum, as would purchase
Eight loynes of Veal, and some two dozen of Capons?

PACHIECO
O strange proportion for five.

LAZARILLO
For five? I have
A legion in my stomach that have kept
Perpetual fast these ten years: for the Capons,
They are to me but as so many black Birds:
May I but eat once, and be satisfied,
Let the fates call me, when my ship is fraught,
And I shall hang in peace.

ALGUAZIER
Steal well to night,
And thou shalt feed to morrow; so now you are
Your selves again, I'll raise another watch
To free you from suspition: set on any
You meet with boldly: I'll not be far off,
T'assist you, and protect you.

[Exit.

METALDIE
O brave officer.

[Enter **ALVAREZ**, **LUCIO**, **BOBADILLA**.

PACHIECO
Would every ward had one but so well given,
And we would watch, for rug, in gowns of velvet.

MENDOZA
Stand close, a prize.

METALDIE
Satten, and gold Lace, Lads.

ALVAREZ
Why do'st thou hang upon me?

LUCIO
'Tis so dark
I dare not see my way: for heaven sake father
Let us go home.

BOBADILLA
No, ev'n here we'll leave you:
Let's run away from him, my Lord.

LUCIO
Oh 'las.

ALVAREZ
Thou hast made me mad: and I will beat thee dead,
Then bray thee in a morter, and new mold thee,
But I will alter thee.

BOBADILLA
'Twil never be:
He has been three days practising to drink,

Yet still he sips like to a waiting woman,
And looks as he were murdering of a fart
Among wild Irish swaggerers.

LUCIO
I have still
Your good word, Zancho, father.

ALVAREZ
Milk-sop, coward;
No house of mine receives thee: I disclaim thee,
Thy mother on her knees shall not entreat me
Hereafter to acknowledge thee.

LUCIO
Pray you speak for me.

BOBADILLA
I would; but now I cannot with mine honor.

ALVAREZ
There's only one course left, that may redeem thee,
Which is, to strike the next man that you meet,
And if we chance to light upon a woman,
Take her away, and use her like a man,
Or I will cut thy hamstrings.

PACHIECO
This makes for us.

ALVAREZ
What do'st thou do now?

LUCIO
Sir, I am saying my prayers;
For being to undertake what you would have me,
I know I cannot live.

[Enter **LAMORAL, GENEVORA, ANASTRO** and **PAGES** with Lights.

LAMORAL
Madam, I fear
You'll wish you had us'd your coach: your brothers house
Is yet far off.

GENEVORA
The better sir: this walk
Will help digestion after your great supper,

Of which I have fed largely.

ALVAREZ
To your task,
Or else you know what follows:

LUCIO
I am dying:
Now Lord have mercy on me: by your favor,
Sir I must strike you.

LAMORAL
For what cause?

LUCIO
I know not:
And I must likewise talk with that young Lady,
An hour in private.

LAMORAL
What you must, is doubtful,
But I am certain Sir, I must beat you.

LUCIO
Help, help.

ALVAREZ
Not strike again?

LAMORAL
How, Alvarez?

ANASTRO
This for my Lord Vitellis love.

PACHIECO
Break out,
And like true theeves, make prey on either side,
But seem to help the stranger.

BOBADILLA
Oh my Lord,
They have beat him on his knees.

LUCIO
Though I want courage:
I yet have a sons duty in me, and
Compassion of a fathers danger; that,

That wholly now possesses me.

ALVAREZ
Lucio.
This is beyond my hope.

METALDIE
So Lazarillo,
Take up all boy: well done.

PACHIECO
And now steal off
Closely and cunningly.

ANASTRO
How? have I found you?
Why Gentlemen, are you mad, to make your selves
A prey to Rogues?

LAMORAL
Would we were off.

BOBADILLA
Theeves, theeves.

LAMORAL
Defer our own contention: and down with them.

LUCIO
I'll make you sure.

BOBADILLA
Now he plays the Devil.

GENEVORA
This place is not for me.

[Exit.

LUCIO
I'll follow her
Half of my pennance is past oe'r.

[Exit.

[Enter **ALGUAZIER**, **ASSISTANT** and other **WATCHES**.

ALGUAZIER

What noyse?
What tumult's there? keep the Kings peace I charge you.

PACHIECO
I am glad he's come yet.

ALVAREZ
O, you keep good Guard
Upon the City, when men of our ranck
Are set upon in the streets.

LAMORAL
The assistants
Shall hear on't be assur'd.

ANASTRO
And if he be
That careful Governor he is reported,
You will smart for it.

ALGUAZIER
Patience, good Signiors:
Let me survey the Rascals: O, I know them,
And thank you for them: they are pilf'ring rogues
Of Andaluza that have perus'd
All Prisons in Castile: I dare not trust
The dungeon with them: no, I'll have them home
To my own house.

PACHIECO
We had rather go to prison.

ALGUAZIER
Had you so dog-bolts? yes, I know you had:
You there would use your cunning fingers on
The simple locks; you would: but I'll prevent you.

LAMORAL
My Mistriss lost, good night.

[Exit.

BOBADILLA
Your Son's gone too,
What should become of him?

ALVAREZ
Come of him, what will:

Now he dares fight, I care not: I'll to bed,
Look to your prisoners Alguazier.

[Exit with **BOBADILLA**.

ALGUAZIER
All's clear'd:
Droop not for one disaster: let us hug,
And triumph in our knaveries.

ASSISTANT
This confirms
What was reported of him.

METALDIE
'Twas done bravely.

ALGUAZIER
I must a little glory in the means
We Officers have, to play the Knaves, and safely:
How we break through the toyles, pitch'd by the Law,
Yet hang up them that are far less delinquents:
A simple shopkeeper's carted for a bawd
For lodging (though unwittingly) a smock-Gamster:
Where, with rewards, and credit I have kept
Malroda in my house, as in a cloyster,
Without taint, or suspition.

PACHIECO
But suppose
The Governor should know't?

ALGUAZIER
He? good Gentleman,
Let him perplex himself with prying into
The measures in the market, and th'abuses
The day stands guilty of: the pillage of the night
Is only mine, mine own fee simple;
Which you shall hold from me, tenants at will,
And pay no rent for't.

PACHIECO
Admirable Landlord.

ALGUAZIER
Now we'll go search the Taverns, commit such
As we find drinking: and be drunk our selves
With what we take from them: these silly wretches

Whom I for form sake only have brought hither
Shall watch without, and guard us.

ASSISTANT
And we will
See you safe lodg'd, most worthy Alguazier,
With all of you his comrads.

METALDIE
'Tis the Governor.

ALGUAZIER
We are betray'd?

ASSISTANT
My guard there; bind them fast:
How men in high place and authority
Are in their lives and estimations wrong'd
By their subordinate Ministers! yet such
They cannot but imploy: wrong'd justice finding
Scarce one true servant in ten officers.
'T'expostulate with you, were but to delay
Your crimes due punishment, which shall fall upon you
So speedily, and severely, that it shall
Fright others by th'example: and confirm
How ever corrupt Officers may disgrace
Themselves, 'tis not in them to wrong their place
Bring them away.

ALGUAZIER
We'll suffer nobly yet,
And like to Spanish Gallants.

PACHIECO
And we'll hang so.

LAZARILLO
I have no stomach to it: but I'll endeavor.

[Exeunt.

SCÆNA QUARTA

Enter **LUCIO** and **GENEVORA**.

GENEVORA

Nay you are rude; pray you forbear, you offer now
More than the breeding of a Gentleman
Can give you warrant for.

LUCIO
'Tis but to kiss you,
And think not I'll receive that for a favour
Which was enjoyn'd me for a pennance, Lady.

GENEVORA
You have met a gentle confessor, and for once
(So then you will rest satisfied) I vouchsafe it.

LUCIO
Rest satisfied with a kiss? why can a man
Desire more from a woman? is there any
Pleasure beyond it? may I never live
If I know what it is.

GENEVORA
Sweet Innocence.

LUCIO
What strange new motions do I feel? my veins
Burn with an unknown fire: in every part
I suffer alteration: I am poyson'd,
Yet languish with desire again to tast it,
So sweetly it works on me.

GENEVORA
I ne'r saw
A lovely man, till now.

LUCIO
How can this be?
She is a woman, as my mother is,
And her I have kiss'd often, and brought off
My lips unscortch'd; yours are more lovely, Lady,
And so should be less hurtful: pray you vouchsafe
Your hand to quench the heat tane from your Lip,
Perhaps that may restore me.

GENEVORA
Willingly.

LUCIO
The flame increases: if to touch you, burn thus,
What would more strict embraces do? I know not,

And yet methinks to die so, were to ascend
To heaven, through Paradise.

GENEVORA
I am wounded too,
Though modesty forbids that I should speak
What ignorance makes him bold in: why do you fix
Your eyes so strongly on me?

LUCIO
Pray you stand still,
There is nothing else, that is worth the looking on:
I could adore you, Lady.

GENEVORA
Can you love me?

LUCIO
To wait on you, in your chamber, and but touch
What you, by wearing it, have made divine,
Were such a happiness. I am resolved,
I'll sell my liberty to you for this glove,
And write my self your slave.

[Enter **LAMORAL**.

GENEVORA
On easier terms,
Receive it as a friend.

LAMORAL
How! giving favor!
I'll have it with his heart.

GENEVORA
What will you do?

LUCIO
As you are merciful, take my life rather.

GENEVORA
Will you depart with't so?

LAMORAL
Do's that grieve you?

GENEVORA
I know not: but even now you appear valiant.

LUCIO

'Twas to preserve my father: in his cause
I could be so again.

GENEVORA

Not in your own? Kneel to thy Rival and thine enemy?
Away unworthy creature, I begin
To hate my self, for giving entrance to
A good opinion of thee: for thy torment,
If my poor beauty be of any power,
Mayst thou doat on it desperately: but never
Presume to hope for grace, till thou recover
And wear the favor that was ravish'd from thee.

LAMORAL

He wears my head too then.

GENEVORA

Poor fool, farewell.

[Exit.

LUCIO

My womanish soul, which hitherto hath govern'd
This coward flesh, I feel departing from me;
And in me by her beauty is inspir'd
A new, and masculine one: instructing me
What's fit to do or suffer; powerful love
That hast with loud, and yet a pleasing thunder
Rous'd sleeping manhood in me, thy new creature,
Perfect thy work so that I may make known
Nature (though long kept back) will have her own.

[Exeunt.

ACTUS QUINTUS

SCÆNA PRIMA

Enter **LAMORAL** and **LUCIO**.

LAMORAL

Can it be possible, that in six short hours
The subject still the same, so many habits
Should be remov'd? or this new Lucio, he

That yesternight was baffeld and disgrac'd,
And thank'd the man that did it, that then kneeld
And blubber'd like a woman, should now dare
On terms of honor seek reparation
For what he then appear'd not capable of?

LUCIO
Such miracles, men that dare do injuries
Live to their shames to see, and for punishment
And scourge to their proud follies.

LAMORAL
Prethee leave me:
Had I my Page, or foot-man here to flesh thee,
I durst the better hear thee.

LUCIO
This scorn needs not:
And offer such no more.

LAMORAL
Why say I should,
You'll not be angry?

LUCIO
Indeed I think I shall,
Would you vouchsafe to shew your self a Captain,
And lead a little farther, to some place
That's less frequented.

LAMORAL
He looks pale.

LUCIO
If not,
Make use of this.

LAMORAL
There's anger in his eyes too:
His gesture, voyce, behaviour, all new fashion'd;
Well, if it does endure in act the triall
Of what in show it promises to make good,
Ulysses Cyclops, Io's transformation,
Eurydice fetch from Hell, with all the rest
Of Ovids Fables, I'll put in your Creed;
And for proof, all incredible things may be,
Write down that Lucio, the coward Lucio,
The womanish Lucio fought.

LUCIO
And Lamorall,
The still imploy'd great duellist Lamorall,
Took his life from him.

LAMORAL
'Twill not come to that sure:
Methinks the only drawing of my Sword
Should fright that confidence.

LUCIO
It confirms it rather.
To make which good, know you stand now oppos'd
By one that is your Rival, one that wishes
Your name and title greater, to raise his;
The wrong you did, less pardonable than it is,
But your strength to defend it, more than ever
It was when justice friended it. The Lady
For whom we now contend, Genevora
Of more desert, (if such incomparable beauty
Could suffer an addition) your love
To Don Vitelli multipli'd, and your hate
Against my father and his house increas'd;
And lastly, that the Glove which you there wear,
To my dishonour, (which I must force from you)
Were dearer to you than your life.

LAMORAL
You'l find
It is, and so I'll guard it:

LUCIO
All these must meet then
With the black infamy, to be foyl'd by one
That's not allowd a man: to help your valor,
That falling by your hand, I may, or dye,
Or win in this one single opposition
My Mistriss, and such honor as I may
Inrich my fathers Arms with.

LAMORAL
'Tis said Nobly;
My life with them are at the stake.

LUCIO
At all then.

[Fight.

LAMORAL
She's yours, this and my life too follow your fortune,
And give not only back that part, the looser
Scorns to accept of—

LUCIO
What's that?

LAMORAL
My poor life,
Which do not leave me as a farther torment,
Having dispoil'd me of my Sword, mine honor,
Hope of my Ladies grace, fame, and all else
That made it worth the keeping.

LUCIO
I take back
No more from you, than what you forc'd from me;
And with a worser title: yet think not
That I'll dispute this, as made insolent
By my success, but as one equal with you,
If so you will accept me; that new courage,
Or call it fortune if you please, that is
Conferr'd upon me by the only sight
Of fair Genevora, was not bestow'd on me
To bloody purposes: nor did her command
Deprive me of the happiness to see her
But till I did redeem her favor from you;
Which only I rejoyce in, and share with you
In all you suffer else.

LAMORAL
This curtesie
Wounds deeper than your Sword can, or mine own;
Pray you make use of either, and dispatch me.

LUCIO
The barbarous Turk is satisfied with spoil;
And shall I, being possest of what I came for,
Prove the more Infidel?

LAMORAL
You were better be so,
Than publish my disgrace, as 'tis the custom,
And which I must expect.

LUCIO
Judge better on me:
I have no tongue to trumpet mine own praise
To your dishonor: 'tis a bastard courage
That seeks a name out that way, no true born one;
Pray you be comforted, for by all goodness
But to her virtuous self, the best part of it,
I never will discover on what terms
I came by these: which yet I take not from you,
But leave you in exchange of them, mine own,
With the desire of being a friend; which if
You will not grant me, but on farther trial
Of manhood in me, seek me when you please,
(And though I might refuse it with mine honor)
Win them again, and wear them: so good morrow.

[Exit.

LAMORAL
I ne'r knew what true valor was till now;
And have gain'd more by this disgrace, than all
The honors I have won: they made me proud,
Presumptuous of my fortune; a mere beast,
Fashion'd by them, only to dare and do:
Yielding no reasons for my wilful actions
But what I stuck on my Swords point, presuming
It was the best Revenew. How unequal
Wrongs well maintain'd makes us to others, which
Ending with shame teach us to know our selves,
I will think more on't.

[Enter **VITELLI**.

VITELLI
Lamorall.

LAMORAL
My Lord?

VITELLI
I came to seek you.

LAMORAL
And unwillingly;
You ne'r found me till now: your pleasure Sir?

VITELLI
That which will please thee friend: thy vowd love to me

Shall now be put in action: means is offer'd
To use thy good Sword for me; that which still
Thou wearst, as if it were a part of thee.
Where is it?

LAMORAL
'Tis chang'd for one more fortunate:
Pray you enquire not how.

VITELLI
Why, I ne'r thought
That there was musick in't, but ascribe
The fortune of it to the arm.

LAMORAL
Which is grown weaker too. I am not (in a word)
Worthy your friendship: I am one new vanquish'd,
Yet shame to tell by whom.

VITELLI
But I'll tell thee
'Gainst whom thou art to fight, and there redeem
Thy honor lost, if there be any such:
The King, by my long suit, at length is pleas'd
That Alvarez and my self, with eithers Second,
Shall end the difference between our houses,
Which he accepts of, I make choice of thee;
And where you speak of a disgrace, the means
To blot it out, by such a publick trial
Of thy approved valor, will revive
Thy antient courage. If you imbrace it do;
If not, I'll seek some other.

LAMORAL
As I am
You may command me.

VITELLI
Spoke like that true friend
That loves not only for his private end.

[Exeunt.

SCÆNA SECUNDA

Enter **GENEVORA**, with a Letter and **BOBADILLA**.

GENEVORA
This from Madona Clara?

BOBADILLA
Yes, an't please you.

GENEVORA
Alvarez daughter?

BOBADILLA
The same, Lady.

GENEVORA
She,
That sav'd my brothers life?

BOBADILLA
You are still in the right,
She wil'd me wait your walking forth: and knowing
How necessary a discreet wise man
Was in a business of such weight, she pleas'd
To think on me: it may be in my face
Your Ladyship, not acquainted with my wisdom,
Finds no such matter: what I am, I am;
Thought's free, and think you what you please.

GENEVORA
'Tis strange.

BOBADILLA
That I should be wise, Madam?

GENEVORA
No, thou art so;
There's for thy pains: and prethee tell thy Lady
I will not fail to meet her: I'll receive
Thy thanks and duty in thy present absence:
Farewell, farewell, I say, now thou art wise.

[Exit **BOBADILLA**.

She writes here, she hath something to impart
That may concern my brothers life; I know not,
But general fame does give her out so worthy,
That I dare not suspect her: yet wish Lucio,

[Enter **LUCIO**.

Were Master of her mind: but fie upon't;
Why do I think on him? see, I am punish'd for it,
In his unlook'd for presence: Now I must
Endure another tedious piece of Courtship,
Would make one forswear curtesie.

LUCIO
Gracious Madam,
The sorrow paid for your just anger towards me
Arising from my weakness, I presume
To press into your presence, and despair not
An easie pardon.

GENEVORA
He speaks sence: oh strange.

LUCIO
And yet believe, that no desire of mine,
Though all are too strong in me, had the power
For their delight, to force me to infringe
What you commanded, it being in your part
To lessen your great rigor when you please,
And mine to suffer with an humble patience
What you'l impose upon it.

GENEVORA
Courtly too.

LUCIO
Yet hath the poor, and contemn'd Lucio, Madam,
(Made able only by his hope to serve you)
Recover'd what with violence, not justice,
Was taken from him: and here at your feet
With these, he could have laid the conquer'd head
Of Lamorall ('tis all I say of him)
For rudely touching that, which as a relique
I ever would have worship'd, since 'twas yours.

GENEVORA
Valiant, and every thing a Lady could
Wish in her servant.

LUCIO
All that's good in me,
That heavenly love, the opposite to base lust,
Which would have all men worthy, hath created;
Which being by your beams of beauty form'd,

Cherish as your own creature.

GENEVORA
I am gone
Too far now to dissemble: rise, or sure
I must kneel with you too: let this one kiss
Speak the rest for me: 'tis too much I do,
And yet, if chastity would, I could wish more.

LUCIO
In overjoying me, you are grown sad;
What is it Madam? by —
There's nothing that's within my nerves (and yet
Favour'd by you, I should as much as man)
But when you please, now or on all occasions
You can think of hereafter, but you may
Dispose of at your pleasure.

GENEVORA
If you break
That oath again, you loose me. Yet so well
I love you, I shall never put you to't;
And yet forget it not: rest satisfied
With that you have receiv'd now: there are eyes
May be upon us, till the difference
Between our friends are ended: I would not
Be seen so private with you.

LUCIO
I obey you.

GENEVORA
But let me hear oft from you, and remember
I am Vitellies Sister.

LUCIO
What's that Madam?

GENEVORA
Nay nothing, fare you well: who feels loves fire,
Would ever ask to have means to desire.

[Exeunt.

SCÆNA TERTIA

Enter **ASSISTANT, SYAVEDRA, ANASTRO, HERALD, ATTENDANTS.**

ASSISTANT
Are they come in?

HERALD
Yes.

ASSISTANT
Read the Proclamation,
That all the people here assembled may
Have satisfaction, what the Kings dear love,
In care of the Republick, hath ordained;
Attend with silence: read aloud.

HERALD [Reads]
Forasmuch as our high and mighty Master, Philip, the potent and most Catholick King of Spain, hath not only in his own Royal person, been long, and often sollicited, and grieved, with the deadly and uncurable hatred, sprung up betwixt the two antient and most honorable descended Houses of these his two dearly and equally beloved Subjects, Don Ferdinando de Alvarez, and Don Pedro de Vitelli: (all which in vain his Majesty hath often endeavored to reconcile and qualifie:) But that also through the debates, quarrels, and outrages daily arising, falling, and flowing from these great heads, his publick civil Government is seditiously and barbarously molested and wounded, and many of his chief Gentry (no less tender to his Royal Majesty then the very branches of his own sacred blood) spoyld, lost, and submerged, in the impious inundation and torrent of their still-growing malice: It hath therefore pleased His sacred Majesty, out of his infinite affection to preserve his Common-wealth, and general peace, from farther violation, (as a sweet and heartily loving father of his people) and on the earnest petitions of these arch-enemies, to Order, and ordain, that they be ready, each with his well-chosen and beloved friend, armed at all points like Gentlemen, in the Castle of St. Jago, on this present Monday morning betwixt eight and nine of the clock, where (before the combattants be allowed to commence this granted Duel) This to be read aloud for the publick satisfaction of his Majesties well beloved Subjects. 'Save the King.

[Drums within.

SYAVEDRA
Hark their Drums speak their insatiate thirst
Of blood, and stop their ears 'gainst pious peace,
Who gently whispering, implores their friendship!

ASSISTANT
Kings nor authority can master fate;
Admit 'em then, and blood extinguish hate.

[Enter severally, **ALVAREZ** and **LUCIO**, **VITELLI** and **LAMORAL**.

SYAVEDRA
Stay, yet be pleas'd to think, and let not daring

Wherein men now adaies exceed even beasts,
And think themselves not men else, so transport you
Beyond the bounds of Christianity:
Lord Alvarez, Vitelli, Gentlemen,
No Town in Spain, from our Metropolis
Unto the rudest hovel, but is great
With your assured valors daily proofs:
Oh will you then, for a superfluous fame,
A sound of honor, which in these times, all
Like hereticks profess (with obstinacy)
But most erroneously venture your souls,
'Tis a hard task, through a Sea of blood
To sail, and land at Heaven?

VITELLI
I hope not
If justice be my Pilot: but my Lord,
You know, if argument, or time, or love,
Could reconcile, long since we had shook hands;
I dare protest, your breath cools not a vein
In any one of us, but blows the fire
Which nought but blood reciprocal can quench.

ALVAREZ
Vitelli, thou sayst bravely, and sayst right,
And I will kill thee for't, I love thee so.

VITELLI
Ha, ha, old man: upon thy death I'll build
A story (with this arm) for thy old wife
To tell thy daughter Clara seven years hence
As she sits weeping by a winters fire,
How such a time Vitelli slew her husband
With the same Sword his daughter favor'd him,
And lives, and wears it yet: Come Lamorall,
Redeem thy self.

LAMORAL
Lucio, Genevora
Shall on this Sword receive thy bleeding heart,
For my presented hat, laid at her feet.

LUCIO
Thou talk'st well Lamorall, but 'tis thy head
That I will carry to her to thy hat:
Fie Father, I do cool too much.

ALVAREZ

Oh boy:
Thy fathers true Son:
Beat Drums,—and so good morrow to your Lordship.

[Enter above **EUGENIA**, **CLARA**, **GENEVORA**.

SYAVEDRA
Brave resolutions.

ANASTRO
Brave, and Spanish right.

GENEVORA
Lucio.

CLARA
Vitelli.

EUGENIA
Alvarez.

ALVAREZ
How the devil
Got these Cats into th'gutter? my pusse too?

EUGENIA
Hear us.

GENEVORA
We must be heard.

CLARA
We will be heard
Vitelli, look, see Clara on her knees
Imploring thy compassion: Heaven, how sternly
They dart their emulous eyes, as if each scorn'd
To be behind the other in a look!
Mother, death needs no Sword here: oh my Sister
(Fate fain would have it so) persuade, entreat,
A Ladies tears are silent Orators
(Or should be so at least) to move beyond
The honest tongu'd-Rhetorician:
Why will you fight? why do's an uncles death
Twenty year old, exceed your love to me
But twenty days? whose forc'd cause, and fair manner
You could not understand, only have heard.
Custom, that wrought so cunningly on nature
In me, that I forgot my sex, and knew not

Whether my body female were, or male,
You did unweave, and had the power to charm
A new creation in me, made me fear
To think on those deeds I did perpetrate,
How little power though you allow to me
That cannot with my sighs, my tears, my prayers
Move you from your own loss, if you should gain.

VITELLI
I must forget you Clara, 'till I have
Redeem'd my unkles blood, that brands my face
Like a pestiferous Carbuncle: I am blind
To what you do: deaf to your cries: and Marble
To all impulsive exorations.
When on this point, I have perch'd thy fathers soul,
I'll tender thee this bloody reeking hand
Drawn forth the bowels of that murtherer:
If thou canst love me then, I'll marry thee,
And for thy father lost, get thee a Son;
On no condition else.

ASSISTANT
Most barbarous.

SYAVEDRA
Savage.

ANASTRO
Irreligious.

GENEVORA
Oh Lucio!
Be thou merciful: thou bear'st fewer years,
Art lately wean'd from soft effeminacy,
A maidens manners, and a maidens heart
Are neighbors still to thee: be then more mild,
Proceed not to this combat; be'st thou desperate
Of thine own life? yet (dearest) pitty mine
Thy valour's not thine own, I gave it thee,
These eyes begot it, this tongue bred it up,
This breast would lodge it: do not use my gifts
To mine own ruine: I have made thee rich,
Be not so thankless, to undo me for't.

LUCIO
Mistriss, you know I do not wear a vein.
I would not rip for you, to do you service:
Life's but a word, a shadow, a melting dream,

Compar'd to essential, and eternal honor.
Why, would you have me value it beyond
Your brother: if I first cast down my sword
May all my body here, be made one wound,
And yet my soul not find heaven thorough it.

ALVAREZ
You would be catter-walling too, but peace,
Go, get you home, and provide dinner for
Your Son, and me: wee'll be exceeding merry:
Oh Lucio, I will have thee cock of all
The proud Vitellies that do live in Spain:
Fie, we shall take cold: hunch:—I am hoarse
Already.

LAMORAL
How your Sister whets my spleen!
I could eat Lucio now:

GENEVORA
Vitelli, Brother,
Ev'n for your Fathers soul, your uncles blood,
As you do love my life: but last, and most
As you respect your own Honor, and Fame,
Throw down your sword; he is most valiant
That herein yields first.

VITELLI
Peace, you fool.

CLARA
Why Lucio,
Do thou begin; 'tis no disparagement:
He's elder, and thy better, and thy valor
Is in his infancy.

GENEVORA
Or pay it me,
To whom thou ow'st it: Oh, that constant time
Would but go back a week, then Lucio
Thou would'st not dare to fight.

EUGENIA
Lucio, thy Mother,
Thy Mother begs it: throw thy sword down first.

ALVAREZ
I'll throw his head down after then.

GENEVORA
Lamorall.
You have often swore you'ld be commanded by me.

LAMORAL
Never to this: your spight, and scorn Genevora,
Has lost all power in me:

GENEVORA
Your hearing for six words.

ASSISTANT, SYAVEDRA, ANASTRO
Strange obstinacy!

ALVAREZ, VITELLI, LUCIO, LAMORAL
We'll stay no longer.

CLARA
Then by thy oath Vitelli,
Thy dreadful oath, thou wouldst return that Sword
When I should ask it, give it to me, now,
This instant I require it.

GENEVORA
By thy vow,
As dreadful Lucio, to obey my will
In any one thing I would watch to challenge,
I charge thee not to strike a stroak: now he
Of our two brothers that loves perjury
Best, and dares first be damn'd, infringe his vow.

SYAVEDRA
Excellent Ladies.

VITELLI
Pish, you tyrannize.

LUCIO
We did equivocate.

ALVAREZ
On.

CLARA
Then Lucio,
So well I love my husband, for he is so,
(Wanting but ceremony) that I pray

His vengeful sword may fall upon thy head
Succesfully for false-hood to his Sister.

GENEVORA
I likewise pray (Vitelli) Lucio's sword
(Who equally is my husband as thou hers)
May find thy false heart, that durst gage thy faith,
And durst not keep it.

ASSISTANT
Are you men, or stone.

ALVAREZ
Men, and we'll prove it with our swords:

EUGENIA
Your hearing for six words, and we have done,
Zancho come forth—we'll fight our challenge too:
Now speak your resolutions.

[Enter **BOBADILLA** with two swords and a Pistol.

GENEVORA
These they are,
The first blow given betwixt you, sheathes these swords
In one anothers bosomes.

EUGENIA
And rogue, look
You at that instant do discharge that Pistol
Into my breast: if you start back, or quake,
I'll stick you like a Pig.

ALVAREZ
—Hold, you are mad.

GENEVORA
This we said: and by our hope of bliss
This we will do: speak your intents.

CLARA, GENEVORA
Strike.

EUGENIA
Shoot.

ALVAREZ, VITELLI, LUCIO, LAMORAL
Hold, hold: all friends.

ASSISTANT
Come down.

ALVAREZ
These devilish women
Can make men friends and enemies when they list.

SYAVEDRA
A gallant undertaking and a happy;
Why this is noble in you: and will be
A welcomer present to our Master Philip
Than the return from his Indies.

[Enter **CLARA**, **GENEVORA**, **EUGENIA** and **BOBADILLA**.

CLARA
Father, your blessing.

ALVAREZ
Take her: if ye bring not
Betwixt you, boys that will find out new worlds,
And win 'em too, I'm a false Prophet.

VITELLI
Brother.
There is a Sister, long divided streams
Mix now at length, by fate.

BOBADILLA
I am not regarded: I was the careful Steward that provided these Instruments of peace, I put the longest
weapon in your Sisters hand, (my Lord) because she was the shortest Lady: For likely the shortest Ladies
love the longest — men: And for mine own part, I could have discharged it: my Pistol is no ordinary
Pistol, it has two ramming bullets; but thought I, why should I shoot my two bullets into my old Lady? if
they had gone, I would not have staid long after: I would ev'n have died too, bravely y'faith, like a
Roman Steward: hung my self in mine own chain, and there had been a story of Bobadilla, Spindola,
Zancho, for after ages to lament: hum: I perceive, I am not only not regarded, but also not rewarded.

ALVAREZ
Prethee peace: 'shalt have a new chain, next Saint
Jaques day, or this new gilt:

BOBADILLA
I am satisfied: let virtue have her due: And yet I am melancholy upon this atonement: pray heaven the
State rue it not: I would my Lord Vitellie's Steward, and I could meet: they should find it should cost 'em
a little more to make us friends: well, I will forswear wine, and women for a year: and then I will be
drunk to morrow, and run a whoring like a dog with a broken bottle at's tail; then will I repent next day,

and forswear 'em again more vehemently: be forsworn next day again, and repent my repentance: for thus a melancholy Gentleman doth, and ought to live.

ASSISTANT
Nay, you shall dine with me: and afterward
I'll with ye to the King: But first, I will
Dispatch the Castles business, that this day
May be compleat. Bring forth the malefactors.

[Enter **ALGUAZIER, PACCHIERO, METALDI, MENDOAZ, LAZARILLO, PIORATO, MALRODA** and **GUARD**.

You Alguazier, the Ringleader of these
Poor fellows, are degraded from your office,
You must return all stolen goods you receiv'd,
And watch a twelve month without any pay:
This, if you fail of, (all your goods confiscate)
You are to be whipt, and sent into the Gallies.

ALGUAZIER
I like all, but restoring that Catholique Doctrine.
I do dislike: Learn all ye officers
By this to live uprightly (if you can.)

[Exit.

ASSISTANT
You Cobler, to translate your manners new,
Are doom'd to th' Cloisters of the Mendicants,
With this your brother, botcher, there for nothing
To cobble, and heel hose for the poor Friers,
Till they allow you pennance for sufficient,
And your amendment; then you shall be freed,
And may set up again.

PACHIECO
Mendoza, come,
Our souls have trode awry in all mens sight,
We'll underlay 'em, till they go upright.

[Exit **PACHIECO** and **MENDOZA**.

ASSISTANT
Smith, in those shackles you for your hard heart
Must lie by th' heels a year.

METALDIE
I have shod your horse, my Lord.

[Exit.

ASSISTANT
Away: for you, my hungry white-loaf'd face,
You must to th' Gallies, where you shall be sure
To have no more bits, than you shall have blows.

LAZARILLO
Well, though herrings want, I shall have rowes.

ASSISTANT
Signior, you have prevented us, and punish'd
Your selfe severelier than we would have done.
You have married a whore: may she prove honest.

PIORATO
'Tis better, my Lord, than to marry an honest woman,
That may prove a whore.

VITELLI
'Tis a hansome wench: and thou canst keep her tame
I'll send you what I promis'd.

PIORATO
Joy to your Lordships.

ALVAREZ
Here may all Ladies learn, to make of foes
The perfect'st friends: and not the perfect'st foes
Of dearest friends, as some do now a daies.

VITELLI
Behold the power of love, to nature lost
By custome irrecoverably, past the hope
Of friends restoring, Love hath here retriv'd
To her own habit, made her blush to see
Her so long monstrous Metamorphoses,
May strange affairs never have worse success.

[Exeunt.

EPILOGUE

Our Author fears there are some Rebel hearts,
Whose dulness doth oppose loves piercing darts;
Such will be apt to say there wanted wit,

The language low, very few Scænes are writ
With spirit and life; such odd things as these
He cares not for, nor ever means to please;
For if your selves a Mistriss or loves friends,
Are lik'd with this smooth Play he hath his ends.

FRANCIS BEAUMONT – A SHORT BIOGRAPHY

Francis Beaumont was born in 1584, near the small Leicestershire village of Thringstone. Unfortunately precise records of much of his short life do not exist.

He was the son to Sir Francis Beaumont of Grace Dieu, and a justice of the common pleas. His mother was Anne, the daughter of Sir George Pierrepont.

The first date we can give for his education is at age 13 when he begins at Broadgates Hall (now Pembroke College, Oxford). Sadly, his father died the following year, 1598. Beaumont left university without a degree and entered the Inner Temple in London in 1600. A career choice of Law taken previously by his father.

The information to hand is confident that Beaumont's career in law was short-lived. He was quickly attracted to the theatre and soon became first an admirer and then a student of poet and playwright Ben Jonson. Jonson at this time was a cultural behemoth; very talented and a life full of volatility that included frequent brushes with the authorities. His followers, including the poet Robert Herrick, were known as 'the sons of Ben'. Beaumont was also on friendly terms with other luminaries such as the poet Michael Drayton.

Beaumont's first work was Salmacis and Hermaphroditus, it debuted in 1602. A 1911 edition of the Encyclopædia Britannica includes the description "not on the whole discreditable to a lad of eighteen, fresh from the popular love-poems of Marlowe and Shakespeare, which it naturally exceeds in long-winded and fantastic diffusion of episodes and conceits."

By 1605, Beaumont had written commendatory verses to Volpone one of Ben Jonson's masterpieces.

It was now, in the early years of the 17th Century, that he met John Fletcher and together they gradually formed one of the most dynamic and productive of writing teams that English theatre has ever produced.

Their playwriting careers at this stage were both troubled by early failure. Beaumont had written The Knight of the Burning Pestle and it was first performed by the Children of the Blackfriars company in 1607. The audience however was distinctly unimpressed. The publisher's epistle in the 1613 quarto says they failed to note "the privie mark of irony about it."

The following year, Fletcher's Faithful Shepherdess failed on the same stage.

In 1609, however, the two collaborated in earnest on Philaster. The play was performed by the King's Men at the Globe Theatre and at Blackfriars. It was a great success. Their careers were now well and truly launched and into the bargain they had ignited and captured a public taste for tragicomedy.

There is an account that at the time the two men shared everything. They lived together in a house on the Bankside in Southwark, " they also lived together in Bankside, sharing clothes and having "one wench in the house between them." Or as another account puts it "sharing everything in the closest intimacy."

This arrangement stopped in about 1613 when Beaumont married Ursula Isley, daughter and co-heiress of Henry Isley of Sundridge in Kent, by whom he had two daughters (one of them was born after his death).

Beaumont, at a very young age even for those times, was struck down by a stroke at some point in mid-1613, after which he was unable to write any more plays, but he did manage to write an elegy for Lady Penelope Clifton, who had died on 26th October 1613.

Francis Beaumont died on March 6th, 1616 and was buried in Westminster Abbey.

In his short life his canon was small but influential. Although he is seen more as a dramatist his poetry was celebrated even then and it continues to gain an avid readership to this day.

It was said at one point of the collaboration of Beaumont and Fletcher that "in their joint plays their talents are so ... completely merged into one, that the hand of Beaumont cannot clearly be distinguished from that of Fletcher." Whilst it was the view then it has not endured into modern times. Indeed, slowly but with certainty the name of Beaumont has been removed from many of their joint works. It has given way to other such luminaries as Philip Massinger, Nathan field and James Shirley.

JOHN FLETCHER – A SHORT BIOGRAPHY

John Fletcher was born in December, 1579 in Rye, Sussex. He was baptised on December 20th.

As can be imagined details of much of his life and career have not survived and, accordingly, only a very brief indication of his life and works can be given.

His father, Richard Fletcher, was a successful and rather ambitious cleric. From being the Dean of Peterborough he moved on to become the Bishop of Bristol, Bishop of Worcester and finally, shortly before his death, the Bishop of London. He was also the chaplain to Queen Elizabeth.

When he was Dean of Peterborough, Richard Fletcher, witnessed the execution of Mary, Queen of Scots. It was said he "knelt down on the scaffold steps and started to pray out loud and at length, in a prolonged and rhetorical style, as though determined to force his way into the pages of history". He cried out at her death, "So perish all the Queen's enemies!" All very dramatic but the family did have strong links to the Arts.

Young Fletcher appears at the very young age of eleven to have entered Corpus Christi College at Cambridge University in 1591. There are no records that he ever took a degree but there is some small evidence that he was being prepared for a career in the church.

However, what is clear is that this was soon abandoned as he joined the stream of people who would leave University and decamp to the more bohemian life of commercial theatre in London.

Unfortunately, his father fell out with Queen Elizabeth but appears to have been on his way to rehabilitation before his death in 1596. At his death he was, however, mired in debt.

The upbringing of the now teenage Fletcher and his seven siblings now passed to his paternal uncle, the poet and minor official Giles Fletcher. Giles, who had the patronage of the Earl of Essex may have been a liability rather than an advantage to the young Fletcher. With Essex involved in the failed rebellion against Elizabeth Giles was also tainted by association.

By 1606 John Fletcher appears to have equipped himself with the talents to become a playwright. Initially this appears to have been for the Children of the Queen's Revels, then performing at the Blackfriars Theatre.

Commendatory verses by Richard Brome in the Beaumont and Fletcher 1647 folio place Fletcher in the company of Ben Jonson, although it is not known when this friendship began. Jonson, of course, was a leviathan of English Literature, so admired that many of his literary friends and colleagues were simply known as 'Sons of Ben'. Fletcher's frequent early collaborator, Francis Beaumont, was also a friend of Jonson's.

Fletcher's early career was marked by one significant failure; The Faithful Shepherdess, his adaptation of Giovanni Battista Guarini's Il Pastor Fido, which was performed by the Blackfriars Children in 1608. In the preface to the printed edition of his play, Fletcher explained the failure as due to his audience's faulty expectations. They expected a pastoral tragicomedy to feature dances, comedy, and murder, with the shepherds presented in conventional stereotypes – as Fletcher put it, wearing "gray cloaks, with curtailed dogs in strings." Fletcher's preface is however best known for its pithy definition of tragicomedy: "A tragicomedy is not so called in respect of mirth and killing, but in respect it wants [i.e., lacks] deaths, which is enough to make it no tragedy; yet brings some near it, which is enough to make it no comedy." A comedy, he went on to say, must be "a representation of familiar people." His preface is critical of drama that features characters whose action violates nature.

In that case, Fletcher appears to have been developing a new style faster than audiences could comprehend. By 1609, however, he had found his stride. With Beaumont, he wrote Philaster, which became a hit for the King's Men and began a profitable association between Fletcher and that company. Philaster appears also to have begun a trend for tragicomedy. Fletcher's influence has also been said to have inspired some features of Shakespeare's late romances, and certainly his influence on the tragicomic work of other playwrights is even more marked.

By the middle of the 1610s, Fletcher's plays had achieved a popularity that rivalled Shakespeare's and cemented the pre-eminence of the King's Men in Jacobean London. After Beaumont's retirement, necessitated by ill-health, and then his early death in 1616, Fletcher continued working, both singly and in collaboration, until his death in 1625. By that time, he had produced, or had been credited with, close to fifty plays. This body of work remained a major part of the King's Men's repertory until the closing of the theatres in 1642 due to the Civil War.

At the beginning of his career Fletcher's most important collaborator was Francis Beaumont. The two wrote together for close to a decade, first for the Children of the Queen's Revels, and then for the King's Men. According to an anecdote transmitted or invented by John Aubrey, they also lived together in Bankside, sharing clothes and having "one wench in the house between them." This domestic arrangement, if it existed, was ended by Beaumont's marriage in 1613, and their dramatic partnership ended after Beaumont fell ill, probably of a stroke, that same year.

At this point Fletcher had written many plays with Beaumont and several others on his own. He seems to have been regarded as quite a talent although it should be remembered that playwrights were required to be prolific, to easily work with other collaborators and to produce work of quality and commercial appeal very quickly.

The King's Men, run by Philip Henslowe, was the most prestigious of the theatre companies and Fletcher now had an increasingly close association with it.

Fletcher collaborated with Shakespeare on Henry VIII, The Two Noble Kinsmen, and the now lost Cardenio, which some scholars say was the basis for Lewis Theobald's play Double Falsehood. (Theobald is regarded as one of the best Shakespearean editors. Whether his play is based on Cardenio or on some other is not absolutely known although Theobald certainly promoted it as his revision of the lost Shakespeare/Fletcher play.)

A play that Fletcher also wrote by himself at this time, The Woman's Prize or the Tamer Tamed, is also regarded as a sequel to The Taming of the Shrew.

In 1616, with the death of Shakespeare, Fletcher now appears to have entered into an enhanced arrangement with the King's Men on very similar terms to Shakespeare's. Fletcher would now write exclusively for the King's Men until his own death almost a decade later.

As well as continuing his solo productions Fletcher was still collaborating with other playwrights, mainly Philip Massinger, who, in turn, would succeed him as the in-house playwright for the King's Men.

Fletcher's popularity continued throughout his life; indeed, during the winter of 1621, he had three of his plays performed at court. His mastery is most notable in two dramatic types; tragicomedy and the comedy of manners.

John Fletcher died in 1625, it is thought of bubonic plague which, at the time, was undergoing further outbreaks.

He seems to have been buried in what is now Southwark Cathedral, although a precise location is not known. There is much made of an anecdote that Fletcher and Massinger (who died in 1640) share the same grave but it is more likely that both are buried within a few yards of each other and that the stone markers in the floor have confused the issue. One is marked 'Edmond Shakespeare 1607' and the other 'John Fletcher 1625' refers to Shakespeare's younger brother and the playwright. The churchyards were, more often than not, completely over-crowded and breeding grounds for disease. Precise record keeping was not a practiced skill.

During the later Commonwealth, many of the playwright's best-known scenes were kept alive as drolls. These were brief performances, usually condensed into one or two scenes and with the addition of music or song to satisfy the taste for plays while the theatres were closed under the Puritans. At the re-opening of the theatres in 1660, the plays in the Fletcher canon, in original form or revised, were by far the most common productions on the English stage. The most frequently revived plays suggest the developing taste for comedies of manners. Among the tragedies, The Maid's Tragedy and, especially, Rollo Duke of Normandy held the stage. Four tragicomedies (A King and No King, The Humorous Lieutenant, Philaster, and The Island Princess) were popular, perhaps in part for their similarity to and foreshadowing of heroic drama. Four comedies (Rule a Wife And Have a Wife, The Chances, Beggars' Bush, and especially The Scornful Lady) were also stage mainstays.

Despite his popularity, and it appears he was held in higher regard than Shakespeare at this time, his works steadily lost ground to those of Shakespeare and to new productions from other playwrights.

Since then Fletcher has increasingly become a subject only for occasional revivals and for specialists. Fletcher and his collaborators have been the subject of important bibliographic and critical studies, but the plays have been revived only infrequently.

Due to the frequent collaborations between all manner of playwrights, and the revisions carried out in later years, having a settled list of authorship to any given set of plays can be problematic. The works of Fletcher and others of this period most definitely fall into this category. It is as well to take into account that during this period theatres were quite often closed either due to outbreaks of the plague or to the prevailing political and moral climate. Printers, anxious to provide materials that would sell, were not above changing a name or two to enhance sales.

Although Fletcher collaborated most often with Beaumont and Massinger, it is believed that Massinger revised many of the plays some time after their original production. Other collaborators including Nathan Field, William Shakespeare, William Rowley and others also can be seen distinctly in Fletchers' works. Many modern scholars point out that Fletcher had many particular mannerisms, but other playwrights would also duplicate these at times so allocating exact contributions of anyone to a play is somewhat of a detective case in many instances. However, from the original folio printings or licensing via the Master of the Revels (the statutory licensing authority to approve and censor plays as well a hand in publication and printing of theatrical materials) as well as contemporary notes a fairly precise bibliography of the works can be given with only a few plays lacking substantial authority and provenance.

PHILIP MASSINGER – A SHORT BIOGRAPHY

This biography was initially written in 1830

Very few materials exist for a life of Massinger beyond the entries of the Parish Register or the College Books, and a few slender intimations scattered here and there in the dedications to his plays. From these scanty sources the following brief memoir is derived.

Our author was born at Salisbury in the year 1584: he was the son of Arthur Massinger, a gentleman in the service of Henry, the second Earl of Pembroke. We must not suppose, from his being thus attached to the family of a nobleman, that the father of our poet was a person of inferior birth and station. In those days the word servant carried with it no sense of degradation. The great lords and officers of the court numbered inferior nobles among their followers. We read, in Cavendish's Life of Wolsey, that "my Lord Percy, the son and heir of the Earl of Northumberland, attended upon and was servitor to the lord-cardinal:" and from the situation which Arthur Massinger held in the household of so high and influential a person as the Earl of Pembroke, we might be justly led to argue rather favourably than unfavourably of his family and his connexions. "There were," says Mr. Gifford, "many considerations which united to render this state of dependance respectable and even honourable. The secretaries, clerks, and assistants, of various departments, were not then, as now, nominated by the government, but left to the choice of the person who held the employment; and as no particular dwelling was officially set apart for their residence, they were entertained in the house of their principal. That communication, too, between noblemen of power and trust, both of a public and private nature, which is now committed to the post, was in those days managed by confidential servants, who were despatched from one to the other, and even to the sovereign;" and, indeed, the father of our poet himself was, we know, in one instance thus employed as the bearer of communications from his patron to Elizabeth. We read in The Sidney Letters, "Mr. Massinger is newly come up from the Earl of Pembroke with letters to the queen for his lordship's leave to be away this St. George's Day." This was an errand which would not have been intrusted to the execution of any inconsiderable person: unimportant as the occasion may appear to us, it would not have been regarded in that light by Elizabeth; for no monarch ever exacted from the nobility, and particularly from her officers of state, a more rigid and scrupulous compliance with stated order than this princess.

With regard to the early youth of Massinger, we possess no information whatever. Mr. Gifford supposes that it might have been passed at Wilton, a seat belonging to the Earl of Pembroke, in the neighbourhood of Salisbury; but this mode of disposing of his early years rests on a very improbable conjecture. It may occasionally have happened that the child of a favourite dependant was admitted as the companion of the younger branches of the patron's family, and allowed to receive his education among them; but this was certainly not an ordinary case; and, like Cavendish, a large majority of the great man's servants and dependants "left wife and children, home and family, rest and quietness, only to serve him."—Massinger was most likely educated at the grammar-school of Salisbury, where many distinguished characters have received the rudiments of their education, among whom the elegant and accomplished Addison is to be numbered. But wherever the first years of our poet's life may have been spent, and whatever may have been the nature of his education, we know that at the age of eighteen (May 14, 1602) he was entered at the university of Oxford, and became a commoner of St. Alban's Hall.

Massinger resided at Oxford about four years, and then abruptly left it, without taking any degree. The cause of this sudden departure is ascribed by Mr. Gifford to the death of his father, from whom his supplies were derived: but Davies relates a very different story, and asserts that the Earl of Pembroke, who had sent him to the university and maintained him there, withdrew the necessary allowance in consequence of his having misapplied the time demanded for severer studies, in the pursuit of a more attractive but less profitable description of literature. Each opinion is equally ungrounded on the basis of any substantial evidence, and rests almost entirely on the imagination of the biographer: what slight authority there is favours the latter supposition, which, perhaps, on the whole, is most consistent with the known circumstances of the case. Anthony Wood, who was born, lived, and died at Oxford; who spent his time in collecting and recording the gossip which circulated in the university respecting the characters and conduct of its more distinguished sons; and whose evidence, however indifferent it may be, is the best that can be obtained upon the subject, confirms the representation of Davies:—
"Massinger," says Wood, "gave his mind more to poetry and romance, for about four years or more,

than to logic and philosophy, which he ought to have done, as he was patronised to that end." This passage corroborates the account of Davies so far as to intimate that patronage was afforded to our author, and that cause of dissatisfaction was given to the patron; but it goes no farther: it does not even state to whom the poet was indebted for assistance, nor that the misapplication of his academic hours was at all resented by the friend from whom the assistance was received: but still Wood is very probably correct in his information that other than his paternal funds were depended upon for maintaining Massinger at the university; and if such was the case, there can be no question from whose hands they must have proceeded; while the simple fact of his having been totally neglected, from the time of his father's death, by the whole of the Pembroke family, till after the demise of the earl, carries with it a strong suspicion that some offence was committed on the side of the poet, and tenaciously remembered on the side of the peer. Henry, the second Earl of Pembroke, died (1601) the year before Massinger was admitted at Oxford; and William, the third earl, to whom the father of Massinger continued attached during life, is universally and justly considered one of the brightest ornaments of the courts of Elizabeth and James. He was a man of generous and liberal disposition; the distinguished patron of arts and learning; and a lover of poetry, which he himself cultivated with some degree of success. It is not probable—it is impossible—that such a man should have allowed the highly talented son of an old and faithful servant of his family to be checked in his course of study, and abandoned to maintain, through the early years of life, a single-handed contest with adversity, for the want of that pecuniary aid which he could have yielded and never missed, unless some strong and decided cause of displeasure had existed. Had Massinger been merely forced to leave the university, as Mr. Gifford supposes, because the funds necessary to maintain him there had failed with the life of his father, we impute an act of illiberality to the Earl of Pembroke which is inconsistent with the whole tenor of his life and character. From whatever source the expenses of our author's education were originally defrayed, their suddenly ceasing argues in favour of the account intimated by Wood and detailed by Davies. If his father had, during his life, supported him at the university, there must have been some reason for the earl's not continuing that support when the father of Massinger was no more; and perhaps the most honourable supposition for both parties is that which represents the earl as offended by the bent of our author's studies and pursuits. By adopting this view of the case we are saved from the painful necessity of either assuming, on the one hand, that a nobleman distinguished among the most amiable characters of his age allowed a highly gifted and meritorious young man, a natural dependant of his house, to languish in the want of that countenance and protection on which he had an hereditary claim; or, on the other hand, that Massinger had incurred the displeasure of his natural and hereditary patron by the commission of some more crying offence.

Every, even the slightest, surmise of Mr. Gifford is deserving attention and respect; but I cannot admit the supposition by which he would account for the alienation that subsisted between the Earl of Pembroke and our author. That distinguished critic has inferred, from the religious sentiments contained in The Virgin Martyr, that Massinger was a Roman catholic, and for that cause neglected by the protector of his father. But if the intimations scattered through this play and others should be received as sufficient evidence of the faith of Massinger, we must, on similar evidence—the intimations contained in Measure for Measure, for instance—conclude that the religion of Shakspeare was the same; and then we are cast back upon our old difficulty, and have to explain why William Earl of Pembroke, a celebrated patron of literary men, and of dramatists in particular, scorned to yield his notice to the catholic Massinger, while (to use the expression of Heminge and Condell) he "prosequuted" the catholic Shakspeare and "his works with so much favour?" There are many reasons for believing Shakspeare to have been a member of the church of Rome; and the patronage afforded him by the Earl of Pembroke proves, that that nobleman extended his liberality to men of genius without any regard to distinctions of faith; but, on the other hand, we have no just grounds for assuming that Massinger really did hold the same opinions. The only evidence we have upon this point, that afforded by the general tone of his writings, is of a most vague and superficial description. What, in fact, can be inferred from it? We may from such a source derive very satisfactory information respecting the sentiments which would be favourably received by the audience, but very little respecting those of the author. The truth is, that though the national religion was reformed in its liturgy and articles, the feelings, prejudices, and superstitions of the people were still almost entirely catholic; and Massinger, like any other dramatic author, writing for the amusement of the people, necessarily addressed them in a language they would understand, and with sentiments that accorded with their own. Besides, as a poet, he would never carry his theological distinctions to his literary labours: Voltaire himself is catholic in his tragedies; and Massinger naturally adopted the creed which was most suitable to the purposes of poetry, and afforded the most picturesque ceremonies and romantic situations. I feel inclined, therefore, to dismiss entirely the theory suggested by Mr. Gifford, for these two reasons; first, supposing our author to have been a catholic, we have no reason for condemning the Earl of Pembroke as a bigot and a persecutor, who would close his eyes to the merits of so great an author, because his faith did not tally with his own; and, secondly, we have no sufficient grounds for supposing him to have been a catholic at all. But with regard to all such visionary conjectures, thinking is literally a waste of thought.

Whatever may have been the nature of Massinger's studies at Oxford, it is quite certain, from the general character of his works, that his time could not have been wasted there; and his literary acquirements, at the period of his leaving the university, appear to have been multifarious and extensive. He was about two-and-twenty (1606) when he arrived in London, where, as he more than once observes, he was driven by his necessities, and somewhat inclined, perhaps, by the peculiar bent of his talents, to dedicate himself to the service of the stage.

The theatre, when Massinger first took up his abode in the metropolis, must have presented attractions of all others the most calculated to excite the interest, and inspire the imagination, of a young man of sensibility, taste, and education like our poet. No art ever attained a more rapid maturity than the dramatic art in England. The people had, indeed, been long accustomed to a species of exhibition, called MIRACLES or MYSTERIES, founded on sacred subjects, and performed by the ministers of religion themselves, on the holy festivals, in or near the churches, and designed to instruct the ignorant in the leading facts of sacred history. From the occasional introduction of allegorical characters, such as Faith, Death, Hope, or Sin, into these religious dramas, representations of another kind, called MORALITIES, had by degrees arisen, of which the plots were more artificial, regular, and connected, and which were entirely formed of such personifications: but the first rough draught of a regular tragedy and comedy—Lord Sackville's Gorboduc, and Still's Gammer Gurton's Needle—were not produced till within the latter half of the sixteenth century, and little more than twenty years before the stage acquired its highest splendour in the productions of Shakspeare.

About the end of the sixteenth century, the attention of the public began to be more generally directed to the drama; and it throve most admirably beneath the cheering beams of popular favour. The theatrical performances which in the early part of Elizabeth's reign had been exhibited on temporary stages, erected in such halls or apartments as the actors could procure, or, more generally, in the yards of the larger inns, while the spectators surveyed them from the surrounding windows and galleries, began to find more convenient and permanent habitations. About the year 1569, a regular playhouse, under the appropriate name of The Theatre, was erected. It is supposed to have stood somewhere in Blackfriars; and, three years after the commencement of this establishment, the queen, yielding to her own inclination for such amusements, and disregarding the remonstrances of the Puritans, granted licence and authority to the servants of the Earl of Leicester ("for the recreation of her loving subjects, as for her own solace and pleasure when she should think good to see them") to exercise their occupation throughout the whole realm of England. From this time the number of theatres increased with the increasing demands of the people. Various noblemen had their respective companies of performers, who were associated as their servants, and acted under their protection; and when Massinger left Oxford, and commenced dramatic author, there were no less than seven principal theatres open in the metropolis.

With respect to the interior arrangements, there were very few points of difference between our modern theatres and those of the days of Massinger. The prices of admission, indeed, were considerably cheaper: to the boxes the entrance was a shilling; to the pit and galleries only sixpence. Sixpence also was the price paid for stools upon the stage; and these seats, as we learn from Decker's Gull's Hornbook, were particularly affected by the wits and critics of the time. The conduct of the audience was less restrained by the sense of public decorum, and smoking tobacco, playing at cards, eating and drinking, were generally prevalent among them. The hours of performance were also earlier: the play commencing at one o'clock. During the representation a flag was unfurled at the top of the theatre; and the stage, according to the universal practice of the age, was strewn with rushes; but, in all other respects, the theatres of Elizabeth and James's days seem to have borne a perfect resemblance to our own. They had their pit, where the inferior class of spectators, the groundlings, vented their clamorous censure or approbation; they had their boxes—rooms as they were called—to which the right of exclusive admission was engaged by the night, for the more affluent portion of the audience; and there were again the galleries, or scaffoldings above the boxes, for those who were content to purchase less commodious situations at a cheaper rate. On the stage, in the same manner, the appointments appear to have been nearly of the same description as at present. The curtain divided the audience from the actors, which, at the third sounding, not indeed of the bell, but of the trumpet, was drawn for the commencement of the performance. Malone, in his account of the ancient theatre, supposes that there were no moveable scenes; that a permanent elevation of about nine feet was raised at the back of the stage, from which, in many of the old plays, part of the dialogue was spoken; and that there was a private box on each side this platform. Such an arrangement would have destroyed all theatrical illusion; and it seems extraordinary that any spectators should desire to fix themselves in a station where they could have seen nothing but the backs and trains of the performers; but, as Malone himself acknowledges the spot to have been inconvenient, and that "it is not very easy to ascertain the precise situation where these boxes really were", it may very reasonably be presumed, that they were not placed in the position that the historian of the English stage has supposed. As to the permanent floor, or upper stage, of which he speaks, he may or may not be correct in his statement. All that his quotations upon the subject really establish is, that in the old, as in the modern theatre, when the actor was to speak from a window, or balcony, or the walls of a fortress, the requisite ingenuity was not wanting to contrive a representation of the place. But with regard to the use of painted moveable scenery, it is not possible, from the very circumstances of the case, to believe him correct in his theory. Such a contrivance could not have escaped our ancestors. All the materials were ready to their hands. They had not to invent for themselves, but merely to adapt an old invention to that peculiar purpose; and at a time when every better-furnished apartment was adorned with tapestry; when even the rooms of the commonest taverns were hung with painted cloths; while all the materials were constantly before their eyes, we can hardly believe our forefathers to have been so deficient in ingenuity, as to have missed the simple contrivance of converting the common ornaments of their walls into the decorations of their theatres. But, in fact, the use of scenery was almost co-existent with the introduction of dramatic representations in this country. In the Chester Mysteries (1268), the most ancient and complete collection of the kind which we possess, is found the following stage direction: "Then Noe shall go into the arke with all his familye, his wife excepte. The arke must be boarded round about; and upon the boardes all the beastes and fowles, hereafter rehearsed, must be painted, that their wordes may agree with their pictures." In this passage we have a clear reference to a painted scene. It is not likely that, in the lapse of three centuries, while all other arts were in a state of rapid improvement, and the art of dramatic writing, perhaps, more rapidly and successfully improved than any other, the art of theatrical decoration should have alone stood still. It is not improbable that their scenes were few; and that they were varied, as occasion might require, by the introduction of different pieces of stage furniture. Mr. Gifford, who adheres to the opinions of Malone, says, "A table with a pen and ink thrust in, signified that the stage was a counting-house; if these were withdrawn and two stools put in their place, it was then a tavern." And this might be perfectly satisfactory as long as the business of the play was supposed to be passing within doors; but when it was removed to the open air, such meagre devices would no longer be sufficient to guide the imagination of the audience, and some new method must have been adopted to indicate the place of action. After giving the subject very considerable attention, I cannot help thinking that Steevens was right in rejecting Malone's theory, and concluding that the spectators were, as at the present day, assisted in following the progress of the story by means of painted moveable scenery. This opinion is confirmed by the ancient stage directions. In the folio Shakspeare, 1623, we read "Enter Brutus in his orchard; Enter Timon in the woods; Enter Timon from the cave." In Coriolanus, "Marcius follows them to the gates and is shut in." Innumerable instances of the same kind might be cited to prove that the ancient stage was not so defective in the necessary decorations as some antiquaries of great authority would represent. "It may be added," says Steevens, "that the dialogue of our old dramatists has such perpetual reference to objects supposed visible to the audience, that the want of scenery could not have failed to render many of the descriptions absurd. Banquo examines the outside of Inverness castle with such minuteness, that he distinguishes even the nests which the martens had built under the projecting part of its roof. Romeo, standing in a garden, points to the tops of fruit-trees gilded by the moon. The prologue speaker to the second part of Henry the Fourth expressly shows the spectators 'This worm-eaten hold of ragged stone,' in which Northumberland was lodged. Iachimo takes the most exact inventory of every article in Imogen's bed-chamber, from the silk and silver of which her tapestry was wrought, down to the Cupids that support her andirons. Had not the inside of the apartment, with its proper furniture, been represented, how ridiculous must the action of Iachimo have appeared! He must have stood looking out of the room for the particulars supposed to be visible within it." The works of Massinger would afford innumerable instances of a similar kind to vindicate the opinion which Steevens has asserted on the testimony of Shakspeare alone. But on this subject there is one passage which appears to me quite conclusive. Must not all the humour of the mock play in The Midsummer Night's Dream have been entirely lost, unless the audience before whom it was performed were accustomed to all the embellishments requisite to give effect to a dramatic representation, and could consequently estimate the absurdity of those shallow contrivances and mean substitutes for scenery devised by the ignorance of the clowns?

In only one respect do I perceive any material difference between the mode of representation at the time of Massinger and at present: in his day, the female parts were performed by boys. This custom, which must in many cases have materially injured the illusion of the scene, was in others of considerable advantage: it furnished the stage with a succession of youths, regularly educated for the art, to fill, in every department of the drama, the characters suited to their age. When the lad had become too tall for Juliet, he had acquired the skill, and was most admirably fitted, both in age and appearance, for performing the part which Garrick considered the most difficult on the stage, because it needed "an old head upon young shoulders," the ardent and arduous character of Romeo. When the voice had "the mannish crack," that rendered the youth unfit to appear as the representative of the gentle Imogen, the stage possessed in him the very person that was wanting to do justice to the princely sentiments of Arviragus or Guiderius.

Such was the state of the stage when Massinger arrived in the metropolis, and dedicated his talents to its service. He joined a splendid fraternity, for Shakspeare, Jonson, Beaumont, Fletcher, Shirley, were then flourishing at the height of their reputation, and the full vigour of their genius. Massinger came among them no unworthy competitor for such honours and emoluments as the theatre could afford. Of the honours, indeed, he seems to have reaped a very fair and equitable portion; of the emoluments, the harvest was less abundant. In those days, very little pecuniary reward was to be gained by the dramatic poet, unless, as indeed was most frequently the case, he added the profession of the actor to that of the author, and recited the verses which he wrote. The distinguished performers of that time, Alleyn, Burbage, Heminge, Condell, Shakspeare, all appear to have died in independent, if not affluent, circumstances; but the remuneration obtained by the poet was most miserably curtailed. The price given at the theatre for a new play fluctuated between ten and twenty pounds; the copyright, if the piece was printed, might produce from six to ten pounds more; in addition to these sums, the dedication-fee may be reckoned, the usual amount of which was forty shillings. Our author appears to have produced about two or three plays every year. Most of them were successful; but, even with this industry and good fortune, his annual income would rarely have exceeded fifty pounds: and we cannot, therefore, feel surprised at finding him continually speaking of his necessities; or that the only existing document connected with his life should be one that represents him in a state of pecuniary embarrassment.

Among the papers of Dulwich College, the indefatigable Mr. Malone discovered the following letter tripartite, which, coming from persons of such deserved celebrity, cannot fail of interesting the reader.

"To our most loving friend, Mr. Phillip Hinchlow, esquire, these.

"Mr. Hinchlow,

"You understand our unfortunate extremitie, and I doe not thincke you so void of Christianitie but that you would throw so much money into the Thames as wee request now of you, rather than endanger so many innocent lives. You know there is xl. more, at least, to be receaved of you for the play. We desire you to lend us vl. of that, which shall be allowed to you; without which, we cannot be bayled, nor I play any more till this be dispatch'd. It will lose you xxl. ere the end of the next weeke, besides the hindrance of the next new play. Pray, sir, consider our cases with humanity, and now give us cause to acknowledge you our true freind in time of neede. Wee have entreated Mr. Davison to deliver this note, as well to witness your love as our promises, and alwayes acknowledgement to be ever

"Your most thankfull and loving friends,
"NAT. FIELD."

"The money shall be abated out of the money remayns for the play of Mr. Fletcher and ours.
"ROB. DABORNE."

"I have ever found you a true loving friend to mee, and in soe small a suite, it beinge honest, I hope you will not fail us.
"PHILIP MASSINGER."

Indorsed.
"Received by mee, Robert Davison, of Mr. Hinchlow, for the use of Mr. Daboerne, Mr. Feeld, Mr. Messenger, the sum of vl.
"ROB. DAVISON."

The occasion of the distress in which these three distinguished persons were involved it is not possible to fathom. We may imagine a thousand emergencies, either creditable or discreditable to the fame of the writers, with which the letter would perfectly tally; but, on such slight and vague intimations, no ingenuity could determine which was most likely to be correct. But from the document a circumstance is ascertained, which, before its discovery, had been called in question. Sir Aston Cockayne, a friend of Massinger, had asserted in a volume of poems, published in 1658, that our author had written in conjunction with Fletcher; Davies doubted this report, but the above letter establishes the fact beyond the possibility of dispute.

Massinger is known to have produced thirty-seven plays for the stage, a list of which is given at the conclusion of this memoir. Sixteen entire plays and the fragment of another, The Parliament of Love, alone are extant. No less than eleven of his productions, in manuscript, were in possession of Mr. Warburton (Somerset Herald), and destroyed with the rest of that gentleman's invaluable collection by his cook, who, ignorant of their worth, used them as waste paper for the purposes of the kitchen.

The great and various merits of the works of Massinger will be better seen in the following volumes than in any elaborate, critical dissertation. If our author be compared with the other dramatic writers of his age, we cannot long hesitate where to place him. More natural in his characters and more poetical in his diction than Jonson or Cartwright, more elevated and nervous than Fletcher, the only writers who can be supposed to contest his pre-eminence, Massinger ranks immediately under Shakspeare himself. Our poet excels, perhaps, more in the description than in the expression of passion; this may in some measure be ascribed to his attention to the fable: while his scenes are managed with consummate skill, the lighter shades of character and sentiment are lost in the tendency of each part to the catastrophe. The melody, force, and variety of his versification are always remarkable. The prevailing beauties of his productions are dignity and elegance; their predominant fault is want of passion.

Massinger's last play—which is unfortunately lost—The Anchoress of Pausilippo, was acted Jan. 26, 1640, about six weeks before his death, which happened on the 17th of March, 1640. He went to bed in good health, says Langbaine, and was found dead in the morning, in his own house on the Bankside. He was buried in the churchyard of St. Saviour's, and the comedians paid the last sad duty to his name, by attending him to the grave.

It does not appear, though every stone and every fragment of a stone has been carefully examined, that any monument or inscription of any kind marked the place where his dust was deposited. "The memorial of his mortality," says Gifford, "is given with a pathetic brevity, which accords but too well with the obscure and humble passages of his life: March 20, 1639-40, buried Philip Massinger, A STRANGER."

Such is all the information that remains to us of this distinguished poet. But though we are ignorant of every circumstance respecting him but that he lived, wrote, and died, we may yet form some idea of his personal character from the recommendatory poems prefixed to his several plays, in which, as Mr. Gifford justly observes, the language of his panegyrists, though warm, expresses an attachment apparently derived not so much from his talents as his virtues: he is their beloved, much-esteemed, dear, worthy, deserving, honoured, long-known, and long-loved friend. All the writers of his life represent him as a man of singular modesty, gentleness, candour, and affability; nor does it appear that he ever made or found an enemy.

FRANCIS BEAUMONT & JOHN FLETCHER – A CONCISE BIBLIOGRAPHY

This bibliography gives the most likely date of writing together with when published, revised or licensed by the Master or the Revels (This position within the royal household was originally for royal festivities, ie revels, and later to oversee stage censorship, until this function was transferred to the Lord Chamberlain in 1624).

Francis Beaumont – Solo Plays
The Knight of the Burning Pestle, comedy (performed 1607; printed 1613)
The Masque of the Inner Temple and Gray's Inn, masque (printed 1613)

John Fletcher - Solo Plays
The Faithful Shepherdess, pastoral (written 1608–9; printed 1609)
The Tragedy of Valentinian, tragedy (1610–14; 1647)
Monsieur Thomas, comedy (c. 1610–16; 1639)
The Woman's Prize, or The Tamer Tamed, comedy (c. 1611; 1647)
Bonduca, tragedy (1611–14; 1647)
The Chances, comedy (c. 1613–25; 1647)
Wit Without Money, comedy (c. 1614; 1639)
The Mad Lover, tragicomedy (acted 5 January 1617; 1647)
The Loyal Subject, tragicomedy (licensed 16 November 1618; revised 1633; 1647)
The Humorous Lieutenant, tragicomedy (c. 1619; 1647)
Women Pleased, tragicomedy (c. 1619–23; 1647)
The Island Princess, tragicomedy (c. 1620; 1647)
The Wild Goose Chase, comedy (c. 1621; 1652)
The Pilgrim, comedy (c. 1621; 1647)
A Wife for a Month, tragicomedy (licensed 27 May 1624; 1647)
Rule a Wife and Have a Wife, comedy (licensed 19 October 1624; 1640)

Francis Beaumont & John Fletcher
The Woman Hater, comedy (1606; 1607)
Cupid's Revenge, tragedy (c. 1607–12; 1615)
Philaster, or Love Lies a-Bleeding, tragicomedy (c. 1609; 1620)
The Maid's Tragedy, Tragedy (c. 1609; 1619)
A King and No King, tragicomedy (1611; 1619)
The Captain, comedy (c. 1609–12; 1647)
The Scornful Lady, comedy (c. 1613; 1616)
Love's Pilgrimage, tragicomedy (c. 1615–16; 1647)
The Noble Gentleman, comedy (c. 1613; licensed 3 February 1626; 1647)

Their Collaborations with Others

The Fair Maid of the Inn, comedy (licensed 22 January 1626; 1647)
The Faithful Friends, tragicomedy (registered 29 June 1660; MS.)

The Nice Valour is possibly by Fletcher revised by Thomas Middleton;

The Fair Maid of the Inn is perhaps a play by Massinger, John Ford, and John Webster, either with or without Fletcher's involvement.

The Laws of Candy has been variously attributed to Fletcher and to John Ford.

The Night-Walker was a Fletcher original, with additions by Shirley for a 1639 production.

Even now there is not absolute certainty on several of the plays. The first Beaumont & Fletcher folio of 1647 contained 35 plays and the second folio of 1679 added a further 18. In total 53 plays.

The first folio included The Masque of the Inner Temple and Gray's Inn (1613), and the second The Knight of the Burning Pestle (1607), widely considered Beaumont's solo works, although the latter was in early editions attributed to both writers. Fletcher himself said that Beaumont was attributed co-authorship of many works that belonged solely to Fletcher or to other collaborators.

One play in the canon, Sir John Van Olden Barnavelt, existed in manuscript and was not published till 1883.

As it is generally thought that on this play Massinger revised them on his own after their initial performances his bibliography has been given separately

PHILIP MASSINGER – A CONCISE BIBLIOGRAPHY

As would be expected many works from this time not longer exist either in part or their entirety. Further many playwrights collaborated on plays or revised them for later performances and we have used the latest position known on each of them for the bibliography below.

Plays written with or revised from Beaumont or Fletcher are given above.

Solo Plays
The Maid of Honour, tragicomedy (c. 1621; printed 1632)
The Duke of Milan, tragedy (c. 1621–3; printed 1623, 1638)
The Unnatural Combat, tragedy (c. 1621–6; printed 1639)
The Bondman, tragicomedy (licensed 3 December 1623; printed 1624)
The Renegado, tragicomedy (licensed 17 April 1624; printed 1630)
The Parliament of Love, comedy (licensed 3 November 1624; MS)
A New Way to Pay Old Debts, comedy (c. 1625; printed 1632)
The Roman Actor, tragedy (licensed 11 October 1626; printed 1629)
The Great Duke of Florence, tragicomedy (licensed 5 July 1627; printed 1636)
The Picture, tragicomedy (licensed 8 June 1629; printed 1630)
The Emperor of the East, tragicomedy (licensed 11 March 1631; printed 1632)
Believe as You List, tragedy (rejected by the censor in January, but licensed 6 May 1631; MS)

The City Madam, comedy (licensed 25 May 1632; printed 1658)
The Guardian, comedy (licensed 31 October 1633; printed 1655)
The Bashful Lover, tragicomedy (licensed 9 May 1636; printed 1655)

Collaborations with John Fletcher and Nathan Field
The Honest Man's Fortune, tragicomedy (1613; printed 1647)
The Queen of Corinth, tragicomedy (c. 1616–18; printed 1647)
The Knight of Malta, tragicomedy (c. 1619; printed 1647).

Collaborations with Nathan Field
The Fatal Dowry, tragedy (c. 1619, printed 1632); adapted by Nicholas Rowe: The Fair Penitent

Collaborations with John Fletcher, John Ford, and William Rowley, or John Webster
The Fair Maid of the Inn, comedy (licensed 22 January 1626; printed 1647).

Collaborations with John Fletcher, Ben Jonson, and George Chapman
Rollo Duke of Normandy, or The Bloody Brother, tragedy (c. 1616–24; printed 1639).

Collaborations with Thomas Dekker
The Virgin Martyr, tragedy (licensed 6 October 1620; printed 1622).

Collaborations with Thomas Middleton and William Rowley
The Old Law, comedy (c. 1615–18; printed 1656).